why food matters

yale

university

press

new haven

and

london

paul

freedman

why

food

matters

Published with assistance from the Louis Stern Memorial Fund.

"Why X Matters" is a registered trademark of Yale University.

Yale University Press books may be purchased in quantity for educational, business, or promotional use. For information, please e-mail sales.press@yale.edu (U.S. office) or sales@yaleup.co.uk (U.K. office).

Set in Adobe Garamond type by IDS Infotech Ltd. Printed in the United States of America.

ISBN 978-0-300-25377-1 (hardcover : alk. paper)
Library of Congress Control Number: 2021933253

A catalogue record for this book is available from the British Library.

This paper meets the requirements of ANSI/NISO Z39.48-1992 (Permanence of Paper).

10 9 8 7 6 5 4 3 2 1

previous works by paul freedman include:

American Cuisine and How It Got This Way (2019)
Ten Restaurants That Changed America (2016)
Out of the East: Spices and the Medieval Imagination
(2008)

In memory of Cecilia Chiang, 1920–2020

contents

introduction

And also that every man should eat and drink, and enjoy the good of all his labor.

—ECCLESIASTES 3:13

Unlike the subjects of other books in this series, food matters because it is necessary for survival. Beyond this fundamental importance, or even because of it, the cultural meaning of food—that it conditions how we see the world and ourselves—is less clear. There is an enduring tradition in Western thought that apart from its obvious biological significance, food does not matter, that it is not an intellectual subject. Eating sustains us and while it is reassuring to expect regular meals, food is essentially fuel and not worth further consideration. In David Mamet's play *Glengarry Glen Ross* (1984) the shady real-estate salesman Richard Roma utters a common opinion: who cares about meals that are over and done with? " 'Cause it's only food. The shit we put in keeps us going. It's only food." The argument of this book is that what people eat does matter for the formation of identity, the preservation of health, the perception of others, and the future of the natural world.

That food does not matter is both a popular and an intellectual opinion. Learned skepticism about food as a serious topic is exemplified by the sixteenth-century essayist Michel de Montaigne who set down what he regarded as an amusing conversation with a chef who seemed to regard his menial job with inappropriate gravity. The Italian cook, brought to France by Montaigne's patron Cardinal Giovanni Caraffa, lectured the philosopher on what he referred to pompously as "the science of eating," affecting "a grave and magisterial countenance, as if he were discussing grand points of theology." Montaigne found it laughable that a mere artisan of the kitchen could describe salads and roasts as if it they merited high seriousness, his discourse "bloated with grand and magnificent words such as one might use in describing the government of an Empire."

Four hundred years after Montaigne's remarks, the distinguished chef Jacques Pépin in his memoirs recollects another dismissal of cuisine as a worthy subject of inquiry, in this case pronounced by a professor of French literature. Having received his BA degree in 1970 from Columbia University, Pépin was admitted to graduate school there and for his doctoral dissertation he proposed to write about food in French literature. His adviser contemptuously assured him that the theme, while certainly novel, was out of the question: "The reason not much has been written on the topic, Mr. Pépin, is that cuisine is not a serious art form. It is far too trivial for academic study. Not intellectual enough to form the basis of a Ph.D. thesis."

No one would dispute the utility of agronomy, physiology, and other science disciplines related to efficient cultivation or physical health, but within Europe and North America, cuisine has not been considered comparable to performing arts such as opera, let alone university disciplines such as philosophy. Recipes and dining out attract popular interest and discussion, but so do many other diversions that do not merit academic attention, from fashion to hang-gliding.

One problem with taking food seriously is that eating is a routine act providing only short-lived satiety; one meal has hardly been finished when the next has to be prepared. Yet just because something is ephemeral does not inevitably make it trivial. After all, before the advent of recording technology, the aesthetic experience of music was fleeting, yet the subject was always regarded in learned circles as a noble endeavor. Beginning in the early Middle Ages, music was a foundational discipline, one of the seven liberal arts. Music has the advantage that its effects are immaterial, spiritual, and in some sense inexplicable. Materiality, necessity, and repetition contribute to the apparent banality of food. Nothing is more implicated in the material world than eating. Ingestion is a quotidian, bodily need, physically urgent, but seemingly not worth extensive discussion any more than is the case for the equally imperious drives for sleep or urination. Many activities are biologically important but uninteresting to humanistically oriented scholars.

And yet, notwithstanding popular and cultivated dismissal, food has meaning beyond its routine aspects, and is important in forming memories and constituting a sense of who we are. Most people retain exactly and fondly the delightful taste and ambience of meals past. Pépin's professor notwithstanding, literary authors *do* write about food, and certain instances, such as Proust's madeleine, are renowned. Far from fading away, enjoyment endures in our minds as entrancing and comforting recollections.

The Covid-19 pandemic accentuated the power of food both to evoke loss and to preserve sanity. During the periods of restrictions, formerly common pleasures such as restaurant dining were remembered with all the more affection because they used to occur repeatedly. In addition, such meals were missed because, as Proust also noted, the only true paradises are those we have lost. Writing from what amounted to exile in Taiwan, the writer Tang Lusun (1908–1985) ended the introduction to a book entitled *Recalling Homeland* (*Guyuan qing*) with the hope that: "If food talk can elicit one's memory of the homeland and then inspire his ambition of recovering the native soil, then I have not written in vain these many years."

Exile, migration, and confinement reinforce the symbolic significance of food. An incomparably agonizing example of the power of food and memory is a cookbook put together by Jewish women imprisoned in the Theresienstadt concentration camp (Terezín, Czech Republic) during the Nazi tyranny. Of course, no one arrived at the camp with a collection of home recipes, and it would not have been possible to find or prepare the dishes remembered for the cookbook while in a situation of near starvation. As recounted in the book *In Memory's Kitchen* by Cara De Silva, the recipes were based on the women's recollections of the comforting, everyday food of home. These inmates were supposedly privileged (the Germans referred to them as *Prominenten*), kept at what was falsely presented to the world as a model Jewish settlement, as conveyed via a grotesque propaganda film in 1944 titled *Der Führer schenkt den Juden eine Stadt* (The Führer Gives the Jews a City). Theresienstadt included Jews of international reputation (among those who survived were the eminent German rabbi and scholar Leo Baeck, the Czech conductor Karel Ančerl, and the Austrian psychotherapist Viktor Frankl), but all the prisoners suffered deprivation and most were sooner or later pushed out for death at Auschwitz and other extermination sites as the endless trainloads of victims choked the camps.

In the face of attempts to obliterate and dehumanize, the Theresienstadt cookbook reaffirmed the Jewish women's identities and personal integrity. Recalling specific foods and how to prepare them constituted a form of psychological resistance and self-preservation. The cookbook is a harrowing document, epitomizing what I hope to show in this book: the significance of food for cultural as well as biological survival. I want to look at this primarily through history, because the significance of food preferences plays out over time and because of the connections between memory and taste.

Not all cultures agree with the Western contemptuous or amused attitude toward dining. In imperial China, poets and other impeccably intellectual members of the elite classes created rhapsodic compositions about the pleasures of the table. Su Dongpo, a Song Dynasty poet and politician, wrote with fond discrimination about cuisine, and there is even a well-known dish, "Dongpo Pork," named after him. One can hardly imagine "Chicken St. Jerome" or "Meringues à la Wittgenstein." The latter once remarked that he did not care what he ate as long as it was the same every day.

The subject of food afforded Chinese scholars an opportunity to reflect nostalgically on personal history, on the better times of their youth. The first-person "familiar essay" (*xiaopinwen*) is a traditional literary genre of self-reflection, often expressing longing for the past. Recalling in poverty the pleasures he had enjoyed during the last years of the recently overthrown Ming Dynasty, the seventeenth-century essayist Zhang Dai lovingly described a "crab club" whose members extensively discussed river crabs during their fall season. Eating crabs accompanied by salted and dried duck, junket, blood clams steeped in wine, cabbage, other vegetables, and fruit: "It is really as though we had tasted the offerings of the immortals come from the celestial kitchens . . ."

There was a boom in familiar essays in twentieth-century China, especially among exiles from the mainland who fled to Taiwan after the communist revolution triumphed in 1949. Culinary nostalgia was a constituent of this literature, as with Tang Lusun's memories of New Year's festival food in Beijing or Liang Shiqiu (1903–1987), who remained in mainland China, recalling the marvelous cuisine in Kunming (Yunnan) where he had lived during the war and to which he never returned.

The Abbasid Caliphate too produced poets who celebrated food and gourmandise and thought leaders who wrote cookbooks. A particularly important genre was formed by "poems of the table," compositions recited in praise of dishes as they were served. Al-Masudi's historical account of the luxuries of the court in Baghdad describes a banquet hosted by the Caliph al-Mustakfī (whose brief reign was 944–946) at which those attending declaimed poems about ideal dishes and the kitchen then prepared them exactly according to specifications. The only thing that proved unavailable, we are informed, was fresh asparagus.

In the Western intellectual tradition, food and drink are eminently compatible with conversation, just not worthwhile as its objects. Learned and convivial table talk is a theme derived from Plato's *Symposium,* periodically revived especially by Renaissance humanists. Accounts of such repasts detail conversations about friendship, arts and letters, and true nobility. Dining together furnished opportunities to display eloquence and wit, but unlike the Middle Eastern or Chinese examples, nothing was said about the banquet dishes and seldom do we even know what was served. The meal was simply a pleasant setting for discourse, not itself worth expatiation.

There are a few exceptions. Learned Greek scholars explored obscure terms for food and dining, speculating about their origin and noting their appearance in literary works. The master of this genre was Athenaeus, author of *Deipnosophistae* ("The Sophists' Dinner"). Written in the early third century A.D., this celebration of cuisine presents an imagined series of feasts, the parade of dishes enlivened by learned talk involving feats of textual recall from the works of poets, playwrights, satirists, and historians about food and pretty much everything else. Here the observations of the chef are treated with respectful attention, although the boastful chef was a stock figure of ancient comedy. Dinner and after-dinner conversations extend over fifteen books, seven volumes in the Loeb Classical Library edition. The *Deipnosophistae* has long been valued for the thousands of literary excerpts quoted by the cultivated diners, the majority of the passages taken from works now otherwise lost. Unlike the usual classical banquet practice, these gourmand-intellectuals talk endlessly about food, discoursing on dozens of species of fish, for example, but also on topics such as the faults of notable philosophers or a catalogue of gluttons beginning with Hercules, or exegesis of the Egyptian custom of serving cakes at human sacrifices. Nothing else in the Western canon equals Athenaeus's often tedious yet absorbing compendium.

Notwithstanding my own affection for prolixity and comedy, I propose in what follows to look at food succinctly and seriously, as both a pleasure and a necessity. I approach this task eagerly, but not as the fulfillment of a life-long vocation for culinary matters. Not until I was well over fifty did I consider food an intriguing subject worth writing about. To be sure, as with many professors and students, I liked restaurants. While some academics are indifferent to food as anything more than an annoying necessity, the majority consider themselves knowledgeable about different cuisines. American college towns have a higher density and greater variety of restaurants than do ordinary cities. In Kansas, for example, Lawrence, where the University of Kansas is located, has more inexpensive and internationally diverse places to dine than the larger centers Topeka, the capital, or Wichita, the state's largest city. Insofar as I thought about food, I used to consider myself in the normal range of faculty of the type who also like classical music or art museums. Belatedly, however, I now recall that when I was ten and my family visited France, I learned the names of all of the two- and three-star restaurants in the Guide Michelin for 1960. A dozen years later, as a graduate student at Berkeley, I was berated by more rigorous peers for going on about cuisine, so apparently I spent a lot of time unaware of my personal trajectory.

My career has been devoted to researching and teaching medieval European history. While studying the social imagery of peasants in the period 1000 to 1500, I noticed how often the upper classes mocked rustic food habits. Consuming porridge, root vegetables, cheese, and on special occasions sausage was a source of satire and amusement, much the way that ethnic minorities in the contemporary world have been mocked for their food preferences. Aristocratic tastes in the Middle Ages were oriented toward game, large fish such as sturgeon, and exotic spices such as cinnamon, cloves, and nutmeg. I wrote a book about the demand for spices in the Middle Ages as an example of class determining culinary taste and the power of seemingly frivolous preferences to launch vast historical enterprises, in this case the fifteenth-century ventures for spices that resulted in the European colonization of much of the world.

Subsequently I wrote about upper-class dining, both in the medieval period and in modern America. Both eras identified certain foods as proof of refinement and so worth showing off. In this book, Chapter 1, "Feast and Famine," reflects this original concern with what different classes consume and the taxonomy of prestigious versus lowly food categories.

Classifying people by their level of culinary privilege or discernment is one way in which food affects identity, how we see ourselves and others. Such associations are not stable but are rather the objects of change and manipulation. For centuries French cuisine defined the tastes of the upper classes around the world, but even though Jacqueline Kennedy was lauded for bringing a French chef and sophistication to the White House, presidents after John F. Kennedy boasted of their plebeian tastes. George Bush, a member of a wealthy dynasty from Connecticut, posed as a folksy lover of pork rinds.

Keeping in mind the importance of both the biological and cultural aspects of food, I hope to show the range and diversity of dealing with what is simultaneously a necessity, a pleasure, and a source of conflict. Eating is a biological imperative, but what we eat depends on preferences dictated by society, not just availability or the environment. The sybaritic poets of the Chinese or Islamic courts were not the only people for whom food is important. Likes and dislikes, recipes, and food experiences form the subject of everyday conversation. Perhaps most significantly, in the future subjectivity rather than science will determine how much progress is made in changing the ominous ecological situation as influenced by food practices. Food production and consumption play important roles in epidemics, climate change, and social inequality. Action on a number of issues, from safeguarding supply to reducing waste, will necessitate changes in attitudes.

The study of food cannot be limited to health and environmental data because people are not swayed by science as much as by emotions, resentments, experience, and other strong but nonmaterial factors. We will look at the objective information about our current situation toward the end of the book, but will expend more space considering those powerful if elusive nonmaterial concerns manifested through how people think about the food of immigrants, women versus men, or according to racial conceptions.

Individuals do not readily abandon the food habits that define them. The French historian of Catalonia Pierre Vilar described a Scandinavian cruise in the early 1950s during which he recognized a group of fellow passengers as Catalans, not just because of their language, but from their scorn for the "Anglo-Saxon" breakfast provided. Characteristic of the Catalans' savoir faire and savoir vivre, according to Vilar, was their ability to persuade the dining and kitchen staff to improvise a version of the classic Catalan *pa amb tomàquet*—baguette grilled and then smeared with olive oil and tomatoes.

Every society makes choices about what is edible and what is not. The classical Greek definition of a barbarian was a nomad speaking an incomprehensible language, but it also included the notion that such people are unfamiliar with cooking. The so-called barbarians, in turn, disapproved of the food customs of the supposedly civilized. For Central Asian herdsmen, fermented mare's milk is delicious, while foreign visitors usually find it nauseating. For their part, the herders regard processed cows' milk as tasteless. What "they" eat, those who are different, whoever they are, is opposed to what "we" prefer. Nationalist, anti-immigration demonstrators in northern Italy carry signs saying "polenta si, cous-cous no!" Polenta, a cornmeal porridge, is a symbol of

Lombardy, although its primary ingredient was unknown before Europeans arrived in the New World and was not adopted in Italy until the nineteenth century. Couscous is identified with North Africa, hence with poor immigrants, but it is also commonly eaten in Sicily. One has to acknowledge that for these northern Italian demonstrators, Sicily might as well be Africa, and in any event, as we know, mere facts are not sufficient effectively to discredit symbols inciting anger.

At the same time, the food of others is often appealing. French cuisine was imitated throughout the world in the nineteenth and most of the twentieth century; Persian tastes and luxuries would influence the gastronomy of many realms and cultures from Hellenistic Greece to Mughal India. A foreign cuisine could be considered in certain respects admirable and in others off-putting. During the 1890s, there was a craze for Chinese restaurants in America, but newspapers popularized the belief that Chinese immigrants routinely ate rats and other vermin, and Chinese food was popularly associated with opium and the so-called white slave trade.

Seemingly benign food choices, whims, and preferences have unplanned global side effects. The routine enjoyment of bananas for breakfast or seafood for dinner is brought about through immense labor, investments in transportation, and at substantial environmental cost. How to move food acquisition and consumption in an ecologically responsible direction requires scientific advances, but also public enthusiasm. Food activists want to change damaging agricultural and processing practices and call attention to the oppressive labor conditions by which food is brought to the consumer. To achieve this requires showing people where food comes from and making them care about it.

Turning the natural world into food has always been difficult, requiring until recently the mobilization of at least ninety percent of the world's population to engage directly with cultivation, hunting, herding, fishing, and then processing and cooking. Even though the average American supermarket contains more than thirty thousand separate items, it is still difficult today to obtain and prepare food—the difficulty is just not as visible. Procuring nourishment involves toil and suffering, but for most of the developed world these remain easy to ignore. The true costs are concealed because only a tiny percentage of the population in well-off countries is employed in anything related to agriculture, and many of those workers (such as the people who harvest crops or work in meat-processing plants) are marginalized immigrants or racial minorities.

The fact that getting enough to eat is laborious is a fundamental starting point for thoughtful consideration of the human condition. According to Judeo-Christian teachings, the Fall made agricultural toil necessary. In Milton's *Paradise Lost,* Adam and Eve tend the Garden of Eden where their work is easy. There is no need to worry about the food getting cold on the table because their vegetarian diet does not involve cooking. In contrast, postlapsarian cultivation is hard, the fields require tremendous effort to prepare and sow, and the harvest is constantly threatened by droughts, floods, weeds, and insects. The Book of Genesis (3:17–19) is clear on this: "cursed is the ground for thy sake; in sorrow shalt thou eat of it all the days of thy life; Thorns also and thistles shall it bring forth to thee, and thou shalt eat the herb of the field; In the sweat of thy face shalt thou eat bread."

Especially prominent in the writings of Saint Augustine is the grim observation that labor in this fallen world usually does not profit the laborer above mere subsistence; agricultural work is a form of exploitation to feed and provide luxuries for the wealthy. Unfree labor might violate natural law, as Augustine and other theologians acknowledged, but they regarded slavery as nonetheless acceptable, even necessary, according to the laws governing society, including Christian society. A modern, secular version of this argument justifying hard agricultural work is visible in the propensity for twentieth-century revolutionary communist regimes, notably in China and Cambodia, to exalt peasant domination by compelling intellectuals to toil in the fields.

Although cooking is not explicitly mentioned in the biblical account of the Fall, it too is essentially a tedious form of labor. In the pre-modern world, without indoor plumbing and with the necessity of using open fires, it took considerable time and effort just to prepare basic foodstuffs, and involved hours of churning butter, or grinding grain for bread, or feeding and butchering pigs. Modern conveniences have alleviated these burdensome routines, but the effort has simply been displaced. Restaurant kitchen work remains for the most part harsh and ill-rewarded in societies such as the United States where (at least before the pandemic) more money was spent dining out (or ordering in) than in preparing food at home. The relatively inexpensive availability of food has also meant a seemingly paradoxical deterioration of nutritional well-being, most obvious in the growing rate of obesity and related diseases such as diabetes.

It is not all bad—against these unfortunate aspects of the current human condition, food remains a source of delight, even a solace in difficult circumstances. In his recent book *The Consolation of Food,* the British chef Valentine Warner marshals stories about culinary enjoyment mixed with grief; his recipes accompany marvelous adventures fishing or discovering a wonderful chef in Crete, but he also poignantly describes cooking escalope of veal with Parma ham for his dying father, who "smiled weakly and attempted to eat a few bites, but could not finish it."

Food denotes joy, frustration, and comfort in the film *Big Night* (1996). The big night in question turns out to be a ludicrous failure for the "Paradise," a doomed Italian restaurant in New Jersey where the wonderful food is too authentic for its customers. Earlier, in a rare happy moment, the normally angry and frustrated chef Primo observes that to eat good food is to be close to God. The movie ends with food as a less metaphysical comfort. Primo's brother Secondo, who has been the front-of-house manager, silently, carefully, and lovingly prepares and serves an omelet to offer spiritual as well as physical sustenance to Primo and to the waiter, Cristiano.

The quotidian nature of eating is a source of tedium, but also of enjoyment. Among the aperçus and witticisms of the diplomat and resourceful political survivor Prince Talleyrand (1754–1838) is this observation: "Show me another pleasure besides dinner that happens every day and lasts an hour." Not everyone is in a position to choose what to eat or able to relax comfortably while dining, let alone to extemporize in a learned and leisurely manner about gastronomy, but neither is the daily pleasure of sharing meals the unique privilege of the elite.

The reason food matters has as much to do with culture as with science, with history as with predictions of the future. The chapters that follow consider food as a biological imperative and an expression of choice and self-presentation. Because the cultural factors are less obvious than the basic struggle for survival, they will be emphasized and discussed as aspects of both pleasure and discrimination: why food is intriguing and meaningful, but also why its satisfactions are so poorly distributed. Food brings people together, but it also serves to differentiate rich from poor, male from female, and to separate along lines of class and ethnicity. Thinking about the significance of food in daily life is an exploration of social as well as nutritional reality.

In 2005, Ruth Reichl gave a series of lectures at Yale University on the topic "Why Food Matters." These talks were inspiring for me at the time when I was just starting to think about food as an intriguing subject. Reichl's emphasis in those lectures on cooking and sharing food as expressive of comfort and communion was particularly striking, but I have also been influenced by her autobiographical books that show the comedy and occasional destruction that accompany a passion for food and cuisine. I hope this book will demonstrate that food matters for the future of the natural world, for ourselves at the present moment, and for the way we think based on past generations' literal and metaphorical cultivation of food.

I feast and famine

He is not a greedy one who is concerned for his next day's food.

—EGYPTIAN PAPYRUS, CA. 50 A.D.

Food's importance is obvious in times of scarcity. The history of civilization is punctuated by famines, some caused by weather (drought being the most common example), many of human origin, especially as a consequence of war. The greatest famine in European history, that of 1315–1317, was the result not of a dearth of rain but of an excess. Unceasing rain in northern Europe ruined the wheat harvest in 1315. Flooding continued to damage crops into 1317, and an epidemic of cattle disease added to the misery. By the end of 1317, about a quarter of the urban population had perished.

Famines were not chronic, but neither were they exceptionally rare. The last great mass-starvation event in Europe started by natural causes was the Irish Potato Famine of 1848, what came to be remembered as "the Great Hunger." The Irish famine, caused by a potato blight, was exacerbated by the British government's callous adherence to a free-market ideology that prevented effective aid and intervention. Although the same potato disease caused malnutrition elsewhere in Europe, only in Ireland did it have such terrible consequences of mass fatality, because nowhere else did people depend entirely on the potato for nutrition. After the Great Hunger, Ireland's population decreased by twenty percent because of starvation and emigration. It is therefore not always possible neatly to separate natural and human causes.

Starvation due to war, of course, continued after 1848. The Second World War's many atrocities created nightmarish conditions of famine, often the results of deliberate human action. At least 800,000 civilians in the Soviet city of Leningrad died of cold and hunger during a siege that lasted from September 1941 to January 1944.

At the present time, governments should be better at mobilizing aid than their predecessors were during pre-modern subsistence crises, but in reality, they usually are not. Among other things the Covid-19 pandemic should teach us is not to overestimate our superiority to past civilizations in the amelioration of human misery. Even in the distant past, political authorities were capable of preventive measures with regard to threatened starvation. Between 1377 and 1452, over half the budget of the city of Barcelona was spent on buying wheat to supply bread to the hungry and to reduce food price inflation and speculation in hard times. The municipal authorities took measures such as increasing storage capacity and developing maritime supply networks that extended as far as Sicily and Sardinia. During food shortages, the urban and royal administrations intervened actively, even frantically, releasing stored wheat, prohibiting grain exports, reducing or eliminating customs duties, ordering bakers to adulterate wheat bread with less desirable grains such as barley, even seizing food supplies from foreign ships anchored in the harbor. These measures were necessary not because Barcelona was poor; quite the contrary, it was because the city was economically developed enough to depend, as we do, on extended and complicated food supply chains liable to spasm and dislocation, as are ours. The good intentions of Mediterranean cities such as Barcelona, Genoa, and Venice were reserved for their own inhabitants, so emergency measures often deprived neighboring regions of relief and assured the spread of panic.

Today in the Global South—that is, Africa, Latin America, and the poorer parts of Asia—food crises may be triggered by natural disasters such as flood or drought, but they become particularly terrible crises because of human factors such as political repression (as in North Korea), war (Yemen and Syria), religious and ethnic persecution (the Rohingya in Myanmar), as well as political corruption and hoarding. Amartya Sen, in *Poverty and Famines: An Essay on Entitlement and Deprivation* (1981), demonstrated that famine occurs because of the oppression of despotic governments or armed conflict, not overpopulation or natural disaster. Apart from actual famine, ten percent of the global population suffers long-term malnutrition, affecting people who are not in the direct path of war or plundered by kleptocracies. The coldly technical term "food insecurity" covers both famines and chronic insufficiencies, the latter due to poverty and maldistribution of food resources.

Hunger is common in the developed world, although not always obvious. Before the recent crisis, twenty-two million public school children in the United States received two free meals per day in school because their parents were unable to feed them adequately. Even families with wage-earning parents often run out of money before the next paycheck, and government programs and charitable efforts are not enough to alleviate the fragility of such situations. The United States Department of Agriculture found that during 2018, eleven percent of the population experienced food insecurity, defined as not having enough money to buy food when it runs out or children not getting enough to eat. In April 2020, the first full month of the pandemic, that figure rose above twenty percent.

Even in good economic times, maldistribution is more obvious than malnutrition, almost grotesquely so: one-third of all fresh food is thrown away, while a considerable part of the population experiences want. Before 2020, Los Angeles and New York had elevated numbers of homeless people, yet both had high-end restaurants with tasting menus for upward of five hundred dollars.

Poverty is the reason why people do not get enough to eat. This might seem obvious, but in fact, since the Industrial Revolution, experts reflecting the interests and prejudices of the comfortable classes have tended to ignore this connection in favor of censuring the nutritional victims for their imputed ignorance and fecklessness. A common lament of technocratic reformers is that if only the lower classes stopped wasting their money on unhealthful or expensive food, they would not be hungry. In the late nineteenth and early twentieth centuries, social workers trying to improve lower-class behavior berated immigrants for preparing spicy or garlicky sauces, pasta, vegetables, and other foods regarded by scientists at the time as nutritionally deficient and by home economists as economically wasteful. Meat and dairy products were deemed more healthful and more American. They were cheaper as well. A nutritionist writing in 1922 bemoaned the fact that with Italian cheese at $1.50 a pound and American cheese at only fifty cents, recent arrivals from Italy seemed unable to realize that the American product provided three times as much nourishment for the same amount of money. The fact that Italians were often sick, according to another well-meaning observer in 1903, was because they stubbornly preferred "innutritious" food that was greasy and full of spices and garlic.

The twenty-first-century version of blaming the poor is to bewail their addiction to fast food, packaged snacks, sugary drinks, and the like. Lower-income people are indeed more likely to be obese and suffer diseases resulting from poor diet, but their ill health is often misleadingly framed as the result of "dietary choices," when it is actually related to price and the *absence* of choice, because healthful eating is relatively expensive. Ramen noodles, Pop-Tarts, canned chili, and fast-food burgers are cheap, whereas fresh vegetables and fish are not. Additionally, the bad options have been made attractive through relentless advertising. The food industry ("the snacking-industrial complex," according to one observer) is intent on maximizing sales of flavorful and profitable products with negative nutritional value, and the government is willing to countenance such items in the name of personal freedom.

One can hardly think that gross inequality is only a contemporary problem. In Matthew 26:11, Jesus says "the poor you will always have with you," often brought out subsequently as a fatalistic reason to ignore them. Some scholars argue that the contrast between rich and poor has a distant but ascertainable point of origin related to the transition from shifting cultivation to permanent agriculture, that civilization itself brought about sharp inequalities. The unfolding of civilization is defined by three discrete but related practices: settled agriculture, living in cities, and writing. Before the creation of early urban centers in the Tigris-Euphrates and Indus River valleys, populations moved around in small groups. Tending temporary gardens and growing all manner of produce, they transferred their location periodically as the land lost fertility. Although they were adept at and dependent on plant cultivation, they were not living for generations in one place and going out to the same fields to grow a staple crop. When it was instituted, large-scale agriculture meant identification of a single source for most calories: rice in China, corn in Meso-America, wheat in the Near East. These provided a steady and predictable harvest in fertile regions with reliable weather—along the Nile River, for example—producing enough calories to feed a settled population.

In these societies, food security increased, in the sense of having confidence that one's food needs would be fulfilled, but nutrition in the first civilizations deteriorated from the norm experienced by hunter-gatherers, because the civilized diet was almost unvaried for most of the population. The ten percent or so who were released from agricultural labor constituted an elite—usually warriors, priests, and administrators—and they enjoyed a varied diet because of the surplus produced by the other ninety percent. Exploitation of subordinated labor made possible great monuments, including vanity projects like the Egyptian pyramids, testimonials of piety such as Mayan temples, and public works on the order of Roman aqueducts and roads. Unequal labor and compensation also facilitated literary, artistic, and scientific accomplishments, produced by intellectuals with sufficient leisure and food security to think and create. Food surplus makes possible cultural efflorescence— although most beautiful artifacts of civilization were expressions not of spontaneous collective enterprise but rather of systematic inequality.

The common people dreamed of something more egalitarian, but for most of history the democratic idea of food security was a fantasy that combined plenty with leisure, a reversal of the curse on Adam and Eve's progeny. In the pre-modern European version of utopia, everyone could eat their fill at any time without even having to bother with cooking. Medieval tales about a mythical paradise called "the Land of Cockaigne" featured fish jumping out of the water fully cooked, roasted pigs running around with knives stuck in their backs for convenient carving, and wine flowing in streams. Here there is no money, no work, and pancakes hang from trees. An American version is depicted in the hobo song "Big Rock Candy Mountain," with its own culturally appropriate references to free stew, whiskey creeks, and cigarette trees. The allure of real earthly paradises was commonly evoked in the nineteenth and early twentieth centuries. Popularized by writers like Herman Melville and Robert Louis Stevenson and painters like Paul Gauguin, Polynesia was presented as a place whose tropical profusion meant food security with minimal labor. Abundant free time was devoted to beauty and sensual enjoyment.

In every society with an unequal distribution of wealth, the popular fantasy of effortless plenty has actually been realized, but only by a small upper class. Even peasants have occasional feasts and celebrations marked by gustatory excess, but historically only the higher orders routinely consumed food in great quantity and variety. Where there is barely enough food production, then a stunning mark of privilege is being able to select what seems most pleasing from an array of culinary options. For most civilizations celebratory dining has been a clear sign of high status. In his cookbook, Master Chiquart, chef for the duke of Savoy in the early fifteenth century, envisages a banquet for five hundred guests lasting two days. Imperturbable, he notes that such an occasion will require at least six weeks of preparation, much of it expended on scouring the countryside for game. According to Chiquart's instructions, hunters with forty horses must set out weeks in advance to acquire and age all manner of wild birds and mammals. In addition, several hundred pounds of spices will be needed, along with twelve thousand eggs. Twelve pounds of gold leaf must be obtained in order to decorate the dishes to be presented at the meals.

Among the recipes in Chiquart's cookbook is one for an edible castle at least six feet high with four towers and a fountain in its courtyard. Atop the towers are displayed virtuoso dishes typical of medieval culinary ostentation: a pike cooked three ways and with three colors without being cut into pieces (tricky); a skinned and redressed swan (roasted then sewn back into its original skin and feathers); a glazed suckling pig; and a gold and green boar's head. Each animal breathes fire by means of a camphor-soaked wick in its mouth.

Fifteenth-century nobles and their chefs loved such aggressively splendid gastronomy. Another example is a feast held in 1478 in Bologna for the marriage of Annibale II Bentivoglio, ruler of that city-state, and Lucrezia of the princely Este family, an occasion that gave rise to numerous eyewitness and retrospective descriptions. The chroniclers are laconic with regard to the food served, but there are long digressions about fireworks, jousting, seating patterns, clothes, and other visual aspects. Every account, though, dwells on one course, for which castles made of sugar were brought out and within each were different cooked animals ready to serve. The dishes were paired with living fauna: birds flew around while their spit-roasted brethren were being carved within a castle; live rabbits and pigs trotted through the hall complementing the simultaneous service of rabbit pies and roasted wild boars.

Ostentation involves waste, although less food was thrown away after such medieval extravaganzas than would be the case at a modern event, because what the highborn guests passed up, the servants consumed, and what they didn't want they gave to their friends and family—and finally a significant remnant went to the poor waiting outside the palace. Local health rules regarding the disposal of cooked food were less strict than they are now. Public opinion accepted lavish entertaining as appropriate for princes, although anger that the gluttony of the few oppressed the many was never very far off and did not end with the Middle Ages.

Belshazzar's feast is the biblical archetype for God's punishment of a ruler's excess. In the Book of Daniel we do not learn anything about the food provided for the one thousand guests at this event, only that they drank wine that the king commanded to be served using gold and silver vessels looted from the Temple of Jerusalem. The festivities were interrupted when a disembodied hand wrote on the palace wall in letters that only the captive Hebrew prophet Daniel could interpret to mean that God had doomed Belshazzar and his kingdom: "Thou art weighed in the balances, and art found wanting." And sure enough, that very night, the realm was invaded by the Medes and Persians, who killed the errant ruler.

Modern autocratic courts, such as those of Joseph Stalin or Mao Zedong, perpetuated traditional banqueting despite their radical egalitarian rhetoric. Stalin alternated theatrical, man-of-the-people simplicity with a peculiar kind of luxury. On one hand, in rustic fashion he would mix two soups and crumble bread into the combination, but Stalin also credited himself with creatively elegant taste. He even invented a fairly complex dish called "Aragvi" (named after a river in Georgia), consisting of mutton, eggplant, tomatoes, and potatoes in a peppery sauce. In addition to his many other alleged talents, all lauded through the cult of personality, Stalin was a gourmet. A lavish but intimidating host who plied his entourage with food, Stalin also ridiculed his cronies and jovially made them taste dishes first to make sure they were not poisoned. These boisterous meals went on until dawn, and were at the center of Soviet power. Foreign minister Vyacheslav Molotov said that the Soviet empire was "truly governed from the dining table," and the disillusioned Yugoslav observer Milovan Djilas concurred: at these dinners "the destiny of the vast Russian land, of the newly acquired territories and . . . the human race was decided."

Ostentatious dining was never a monopoly of princes and despots. Just after the conclusion of the American Civil War, a spectacular dinner was offered by the English railway and construction magnate Sir Morton Peto for 250 guests at Delmonico's in New York, generally acknowledged as the finest restaurant in the country. The cost was two hundred dollars per person—an astronomical amount at a time when the average wage was five dollars a week. There were ten courses with thirty-eight separate dishes, including such difficult creations as *cassolettes de foie-gras, chaudfroid de rouge-gorges à la Bohémienne,* and *buisson de ris d'agneau Pascaline.* In almost biblical fashion—not quite overnight, but in less than two years—Sir Morton's railroad speculations unraveled, and he was declared bankrupt.

Celebratory excess characterizes our current Gilded Age as well. The global plutocracy organizes spectacular parties, although the emphasis is not on food but on other types of spectacle: celebrity performances—Rod Stewart singing for the private equity billionaire Stephen Schwarzman in 2007—or vulgar, non-gastronomic displays, as at the birthday party thrown by the criminal business executive Dennis Kozlowski at which an ice sculpture modeled on Michelangelo's *David* spouted vodka from its penis. At least this latter has an historical pedigree. At a great banquet in 1454 known as "The Feast of the Pheasant," held to promote a crusade against the Turks, the duke of Burgundy ordered a statue of a female figure placed near the tables, and from her breasts spiced wine flowed throughout the meal.

What rich people actually like to eat depends not only on time and place, but on just how rich, the difference between what would now be the top five percent versus the top .01 percent. The distinction between high-level gourmandise and merely dining well is evident at different periods: in the Middle Ages, the aristocracy consumed vast amounts of spices that had to be imported from distant and virtually unknown lands, from India and even farther east. Large, succulent fish like sturgeon, or unusual ones such as lamprey, which tastes like meat and so was particularly prized in Lent, were de rigueur for princely tables. The well-off burghers, more interested in plenty and good fellowship than esoteric prestige, consumed charcuterie, salted herring, and cheese, all tasty but thrifty, cured foods shunned by the nobles. The commercial elite did not share the aristocrats' objection to lowly vegetables such as turnips or cabbage, and they drank beer as well as wine.

Anybody with money can eat well, but it requires taste and a certain fashionable knowledge to show off effectively. The food of the truly wealthy, not the merely affluent, has always been oriented toward prestige and rarity. Recherché foods such as ortolans, caviar, and truffles in Europe, birds' nests, or shark-fin in China, have demonstrated upper-class status and the ability to spend extravagantly on unique tastes.

Alternatively, it is possible to convert sobriety and abstemiousness into marks of distinction, so that today in some affluent circles, health and thinness are valued more than appreciation of food. Self-denial has always been a measure of distinction for pious and intellectual figures, but now it is associated with entrepreneurial or leadership behavior, not just religious or secular ascetics such as the Saint Theresas or Wittgensteins of this world. Gastronomic restraint has been advocated by figures from the comfortable classes, such as Benjamin Franklin ("eat to live, don't live to eat"). More recently, General Stanley A. McChrystal boasted that he only ate twice a day, since meals were a waste of time, a sentiment recalling the observation by Michael Douglas in the movie *Wall Street* (1987): "Lunch is for wimps." Symbolic representation of the relationship between wealth and food has changed from the ostentatious to the self-denying; from the gluttonous Diamond Jim Brady or King Edward VII at the turn of the twentieth century to the frugal Warren Buffett and the faddish Steve Jobs of our era.

More often, however, preoccupation with elaborate meals is regarded as an upper-class vice, a form of overweening, often ludicrous ostentation. Near the end of Mozart's *Don Giovanni,* just before the statue shows up for dinner to drag the libertine down to hell, Don Giovanni is feasting while his servant Leporello remarks on his master's "barbarous appetite." Sometimes it is the lower orders who are depicted as opportunistically gluttonous even if their ordinary diet is meager. Medieval and Renaissance drawings and paintings of peasant festivities show dogs running off with strings of sausages and inebriated celebrants vomiting from consuming too much food and drink. Those dogs not occupied in dragging around sausages are licking up the vomit.

Even if the wealthy are portrayed as greedy, a complementary theme is that food is less important to those of spiritual or imaginative delicacy than to ordinary people, immersed as they are in unthinking physical immediacy. Once again, *Don Giovanni:* during the epilogue, now that the vicious nobleman has been punished, the three wronged women of different social classes announce their plans. The anguished aristocrat Donna Anna will wait a year before marrying the importunate Don Ottavio so that her heart can heal from her father's murder at the hands of Don

Giovanni. Donna Elvira, representing middle-class sensitivity, has been so afflicted by recent experience that she intends to enter a convent, there to await the end of her life. Neither Anna nor Elvira appears to be interested in her next meal. By contrast, the rustic couple Zerlina and Masetto cheerfully announce they are going home for dinner.

It is safe to assume that the newlywed peasants in *Don Giovanni* will sit down to a modest if satisfying meal. This does not suffice for the upper classes, who demand culinary distinction. The forms such distinction take might include rarity of primary products, skill required in cooking, or special effects such as flaming or sugar sculptures. In pre-modern civilizations, exoticism and the distance ingredients had to travel were paramount in denoting high status. During the European Middle Ages, spices enjoyed great prestige, benefiting from the mystery of their far-off Asiatic origins. Before Marco Polo's report of his voyages circulated at the beginning of the fourteenth century, no one in Europe had a clear idea of where spices like nutmeg or ginger came from, only that they grew in a magical land called "India" whose exotic allure increased their value. Even when geographical knowledge had improved, in eighteenth-century Europe, pineapples and sea turtles were marvelous delicacies that had to be imported from far-off territories, assuring that their arrival in decent condition was logistically complicated. In Alexandre Dumas's *The Count of Monte Cristo* (published between 1844 and 1846), the Count serves a unique meal that exemplifies the taste of the wealthy for what is difficult to obtain. At a splendid ("oriental") feast, the Count presents a lamprey from Lake Fusaro in southern Italy and a sterlet (a type of sturgeon) from the Volga. Given their particular habitats, this must be the first time fresh lamprey and sterlet were served at the same meal. Both creatures had been kept alive during their long journeys by means of casks furnished with water and appropriate food. As an additional extravagance, *two* of each were packed in case one died en route.

Because modern transport and refrigeration now make distance less of an obstacle, little social cachet is attached anymore to consuming things from far away; most people in the developed world have no trouble obtaining bananas, cinnamon, chocolate, and other tropical products. Paradoxically, today it is the local and seasonal that confers distinction. In New York, spring asparagus from New Jersey or the Hudson River valley is worth boasting about, as opposed to asparagus from Peru, available all year at a cheaper price. Distance is prestigious only if it enhances authenticity and the perception of quality, so olive oil from Italy remains more sought-after than that of California, and Caspian Sea caviar is more esteemed than other versions.

Exoticism alone is not sufficient to give a particular food item cachet—there is as yet little demand for insects. But if the criteria of prestige have changed over time, gastronomic discrimination still confers social capital. The point of being wealthy is to show that you are wealthy, and part of that demonstration is through food.

Given the ability of well-off people to command so many kinds of food, it is surprising how often their tastes return to the same high-prestige items. For over a century, caviar, pâté de foie gras, and truffles have appeared with obsessive frequency on menus designed for people of means and discernment. We can see this kind of repetition in 269 menus of elaborate dinners served to twelve distinguished men in New York City who in 1868 formed the Zodiac Club, with each member identified by an astrological sign. They dined together six times a year, usually at clubs, and published the menus of their dinners held between 1868 and 1915. Oysters started eighty-five percent of the repasts; saddle of lamb or mutton appeared in more than half; terrapin (a species of turtle) in just less than half. Wild canvasback duck was also a frequent repeat. The twentieth-century menus were a little simpler, but the founders would have found comfortingly familiar the last menus of 1915 in the published series.

Zodiac initiates were people like J. P. Morgan who could afford anything, and because this was a dining society without guests or charitable, political, or institutional purpose, the meals were the center of attention. Certain items were ubiquitous because the club members actually enjoyed them, but also because they were signs of wealth. In the minutes of the club's meetings no one is recorded as complaining, "saddle of mutton . . . again?" Perhaps this is simply an aspect of the dilemma often faced when ordering a restaurant meal: should you decide for what you know you like, or do you prefer experimentation? Because their dinners ran to as many as twelve courses, Zodiac members could expect familiar dishes and also try new ones. The surviving menus list 129 different entrées. One would reassuringly begin the meal with predictable oysters and look forward to the nearly inevitable appearance of mutton or terrapin, but entrées such as boneless squab *à l'ancien,* or *pâté de foie gras en croûte* would be new diversions.

Between the extremes of poverty and luxury, there is a considerable territory of mid-level sustenance. A sensible form of *joie de vivre* stands between renunciation and ostentation, between the meager diet of the poor and the overweening greed of the rich. In about 1470, the scholar Bartolomeo Sacchi, known to his friends as "Platina," published in Rome a learned cookbook entitled *On Right Pleasure and Good Health* (*De honeste voluptate et valetudine*), a notable exception to the rule that Western intellectuals did not consider food a worthy field of study. This was a great success and there are at least five further incunable editions. In keeping with the general contempt for gastronomy evinced by scholars, Platina was retrospectively criticized for his inappropriate hobby. In the satiric *Ragguagli di Parnaso* ("Newsletter from Parnassus"), published in 1612, the author Traiano Boccalini has Platina chastised by Apollo for frequenting food shops instead of libraries. The god, patron of literature and music, pronounces, "there is no fouler defect nor vice, than to study how to please the palate."

This was certainly unfair, for Sacchi, a prominent Roman humanist, edited classical texts, wrote extensively on politics, history, honor, and morality, and was appointed the Vatican librarian by Pope Sixtus IV in 1475. His cookbook title reflects classical philosophers' praise of moderation, although the reader of today will be unlikely to consider the recipes austere. True, Platina does discuss simple fare such as millet and broad beans, and he laments the aversion of the wealthy to vegetables. He denounces luxury, claiming that he and his friends are content with plebeian onions and garlic, but he nevertheless gives instructions for making elaborate pies, sow's udder and tongue, and Catalan-style partridge. The first recipe in the book is for peacock, which Platina admits is adored by nouveaux riches.

The United States, rather than adhering to the classical restraint recommended by *De honeste voluptate,* has tended to oscillate between rigid morality and gross materialism. Often these occur simultaneously. Americans in the 1920s banned alcohol, thus creating an illegal industry out of it; the current scene witnesses successive dietary fads along with widespread obesity. This country has found it hard to experience measured pleasure in quality rather than opting for over-ascetic nutritionism, which sets aside enjoyment in the name of health claims, or at the other extreme, routine gluttony as exemplified by restaurant portion size or the ubiquity of sugar.

What we eat, if we are fortunate to be presented with choices, is not just a form of affluent display or social conformity. There is more to dining well than showing off. It is important to defend the assertion that *good* food matters, "good" defined not in terms of whatever currently passes for nutritional guidance, but as food that tastes wonderful. Realizing that appreciation of cuisine does not have to be a snobbish affair is the best result of what has been termed the California Food Revolution that began in the 1970s. A goal of that upheaval was to make food delightful, not merely functional. Its impetus came from France, Italy, and other parts of Europe where local ingredients and dishes are cherished and dining is a quotidian but important pleasure, not an irritating distraction from business. Revolutionary as it was, this movement essentially reasserted the teachings of moderate, well-chosen enjoyment.

James Beard, M. F. K. Fisher, Julia Child, and Alice Waters were among a group of American postwar "food influencers" who found in France a way of life in which dining was not only better in quality than in the United States but a central part of civilized *joie de vivre.* Admiration of French culinary culture was hardly novel, as France for over three centuries had determined haute cuisine for the rest of the world. Applying the lessons of French attitudes in the United States was new, however, and it meant focusing on ingredients and defining quality in terms of flavor and intensity. In the 1970s, when it was easier to find Brazilian hearts of palm in a can or Indian chutney in a jar than a ripe peach or a tomato with some actual taste, the assertion of flavor and freshness was a subversive act. Following the French example, culinary revolutionaries promoted quality according to seasonality and locale: enjoying New Jersey tomatoes in August rather than consuming tasteless hard tomatoes year-round.

In many parts of the world during the 1970s and 1980s the ability to buy tropical or out-of-season produce was still a special treat or new. The East German authorities, normally unable to organize a reliable supply of fresh produce, made sure that oranges imported from Cuba were available at Christmas. The appearance of non-seasonal fruit and vegetables in China was a sign of its surging prosperity beginning in the late 1980s.

The American turn toward what now is called farm-to-table has many points of origin, but the best known are in California. Chez Panisse, the restaurant in Berkeley opened by Alice Waters in 1971, is often presented as the beginning of the food revolution, but it had plenty of company. Informality, rustic cuisine, Mediterranean or Mexican rather than narrowly French orientation—such innovations were tried out at restaurants like Zuni in San Francisco, Fourth Street Grill in Berkeley, and Spago and Michael's in the Los Angeles area. In the East, the Canal House in upstate New York and Hubert's and La Chanterelle in New York City exemplified these trends. The rediscovery of heartiness and spice in the late 1970s and early 1980s owes a lot to southern Louisiana's Paul Prudhomme.

What was unusual about Alice Waters was using food to reform society. Redirecting American tastes away from bland packaged homogenization toward locavore, seasonal gastronomic pleasure was not intended as a gesture of social exclusivity, but rather proposed as an insurrectionary act against corporate gigantism. Chez Panisse exemplified a hippie critique of mainstream food consumption, but in place of countercultural indifference to culinary delight, Waters considered it her mission to create food that was delicious, not renunciatory. Instead of eating brown rice and seaweed because they are virtuous, one could experience healthful *and* sensuous enjoyment, which, as Platina long ago observed, should be complementary, not opposed. Despite her exemplary left-wing credentials, Waters vigorously denied that taking pleasure in food is a form of wasteful consumerism, or that advocating culinary enjoyment was only for reactionary snobs. Pleasure, in her estimation, defies the reigning functionalist values that place the machine of economic productivity above the human being.

It is useful to set Frances Moore Lappé's *Diet for a Small Planet* (1971) alongside Michael Pollan's *In Defense of Food: An Eater's*

Manifesto (2008) and Alice Waters's autobiography, *Coming to My Senses: The Making of a Counterculture Cook* (2017). Lappé vigorously took issue with the accepted Malthusian idea among ecologists that population would soon outstrip the world's agricultural production. There was more than enough food for everyone, she argued, if prioritized and distributed properly. Lappé advanced what then was a radical, almost absurd idea that because so much grain and fertile land was consumed by livestock rearing, eating vegetables instead of meat would relieve the global food supply problem.

The world would be a considerably better place if Lappé's prescriptions, now fifty years old, had been followed. With events like the first Earth Day in 1970, the decade of the seventies gave birth to worldwide activism, ancestor of today's concern with sustainability. The organic food movement took off as well: more than three hundred organic cookbooks were published between 1970 and 1980, compared with just fifteen between 1940 and 1970.

Diet for a Small Planet was a bestseller, and the term ". . . for a small planet" became a formula, a mantra, applied to a variety of situations. Unfortunately, this virtuous agenda remained the property of a niche dismissed by mainstream opinion as comprising back-to-the-land, granola-eating, flannel-shirt-wearing tree huggers. Organic products today account for four percent of all food sales— significant, but unimpressive given how long ago environmental problems and their food-related solutions were first identified.

One factor limiting the impact of *Diet for a Small Planet* was that Lappé was cavalier about whether or not the food she proposed tasted any good. Her rejoinder to criticism was that people would simply have to get used to the recommended dietary regimen, finding their own satisfactory repertoire from the permitted items. Some popular restaurants such as Moosewood in Ithaca, New York (established in 1973), presented attractive, multiethnic vegetarian options, and this particular restaurant and its cookbooks have become legendary. Nevertheless, as long as a healthful and planet-sustainable diet was perceived as renunciatory, its adoption was limited to an enlightened minority.

By the time of Michael Pollan's *In Defense of Food,* the notion that virtuous food should be appealing was widely accepted. Very much in line with Platina, Pollan advocates moderation in attitudes toward food and its consumption. His common-sense approach is encapsulated in the formula "Eat food. Not too much. Mostly plants." The first dictum is not as obvious as it might seem, because Pollan distinguishes between food and food-like substances with no or negative nutritive value, things like yogurt from a tube or Cheez Whiz. He also condemns health marketing that deprives food of flavor, such as tasteless lean pork advertised as "the new white meat."

Like Lappé and Pollan, Alice Waters thinks that decisions about what to eat have consequences that can change the world. As her book title *Coming to My Senses: The Making of a Counterculture Chef* implies, her attitude toward food combines radical reform with sensuality, a reworking of a 1960s dissident argument that pleasure will subvert a society mesmerized by war, state power, and useless overproduction.

Waters and other chefs have turned much of their attention to environmental crises, particularly those exacerbated or brought on by climate change. Warnings of catastrophic unsustainability have been around for decades, and there is a long history of their apparent error and humanity's ability to evade dire predictions. In 1980, Paul Ehrlich, the best-known overpopulation alarmist, made a bet with the economist Julian Simon that within a decade the price of five strategic metals, proxies for the relationship between demographic growth and demand, would increase. In fact, over the next ten years they declined fifty-seven percent in value, and Ehrlich lost his bet. Technology, human ingenuity, innovation, and new economic incentives held off what seemed to be inevitable reckoning. As we are seeing, however, with fires in Australia and the American West, floods and hurricanes in Bangladesh and the Caribbean, and other climate-related shifts, this time something is occurring that is beyond an immediate fix. Rather than overpopulation, climate shifts are already causing nightmarish scenarios of hunger, displacement, the destruction of nature, and political upheaval. Climate disruption and consequent migration are likely to destabilize both the price and the availability of what is at the moment a surplus of food in the global North. In such a world feast and famine will continue to coincide, only even more disturbingly than now.

2 religious rules and gastronomic identity

Labor not for the meat which perisheth, but for the meat that endureth unto everlasting life . . .

—JOHN 6:27

Food matters spiritually. Faith teachings often proscribe certain foods such as pork, or onions, but exalt other foods and rituals as holy. What is forbidden in one set of religious practices might be sacred in another: wine is not permitted to Muslims, but it is part of the Catholic Eucharist and figured in the worship of Greek and Roman deities. In the religious imagination, eating is linked to this-worldly life and embodiment. Some foods can be considered corrupting or polluting, but meals and other forms of ceremonial consumption of food are sacred, connected with a higher eternal order.

What are culinary rules for? Those of a secular orientation often look on religious dietary laws as arbitrary or superstitious. At best, such regulation may be seen as functional. A common, although unconvincing, example of functionalism is the notion that Jewish prohibitions were based on insight into the danger of trichinosis, a disease spread by worms in contaminated pork. Not only is there no evidence for this, but the laws of kashrut go well beyond forbidding pork and extend to regulating animal slaughtering and meat preparation.

Religions impose food restrictions with different justifications: as penance (strong in Christianity), or as a form of ascetic but self-enhancing observance (the Islamic month of Ramadan), to prevent sacrilege or pollution (Jewish or Hindu regulations), or to avoid killing animals (Jains, Buddhists). The different teachings about diet can be categorized into negative and positive. The negative meaning centers on trespass, the consequences of disobedience to God's ordinances, but also the horror the faithful feel for the act of eating something impermissible. For some people and under certain circumstances culinary trespassing can be attractive. Religious adherents experience temptation to try prohibited foods that they see their infidel neighbors routinely enjoying, but more frequently such indulgence is abhorrent. The very idea of tasting these things evokes an instinctual disgust learned in childhood.

On the other hand, you do not have to be religiously inclined to feel visceral food revulsion. Most Americans today are repelled by organ meat or peripheral animal parts such as chicken feet or hog jowl. This is not a permanent cultural fact—elegant restaurants in nineteenth-century America routinely served delicacies such as calf's head in brain sauce or pig's feet with sauce poulette to an enthusiastic public. Organ meat came to be associated with poverty, but so were cornbread and molasses or baked beans, but these never evoked a stomach-turning response from the prosperous.

Positive forms of religious fasting are weaker than the negative aspects of penance and obedience; thus a sense of spiritual benefit tends to be less important than fears of spiritual pollution. Nevertheless, there are some examples of the idea that food constraints make one a better person. Vegetarianism, a tenet of Buddhism and a practice embraced by segments of Indian society, can be experienced as a contemplative form of self-care. The Abrahamic religions don't take quite this approach except to the extent that Islam combines negative and positive, regarding Ramadan fasting as a form of discipline, of deprivation punctuated by the daily (if delayed) joy of breaking the fast when the sun sets. Nebulous New Age spirituality focuses on fasting as a form of cleansing, of detoxification. Nutritive deprivation functions as secular penance with a desired result of lightness, release, or focus.

New Age religious sentiment gets rid of the direct penitential aspect of fasting in favor of centering and restoration of equilibrium. Traditionally, however, religious teachings were less intent on self-improvement and more concerned with atonement. Meat has been particularly susceptible to regulations or prohibitions. In the medieval Christian world, monastic rules forbade meat except in rare circumstances, such as illness, for which meat-eating was deemed therapeutic. Hindu practices offer varying dietary regimes depending on caste, region, and vocation. The Brahmins as a priestly caste are more likely to be vegetarian, but geographical variation means that relatively few Kashmiri or Bengali Brahmins abstain from meat. In certain parts of India, a majority practices vegetarianism and also might avoid garlic and onions. In Gujarat, sixty-nine percent of the population is vegetarian, whereas in Kerala the figure is only six percent.

Followers of the Buddhist and Jain faiths abstain from meat for moral reasons, believing that it is wrong to kill animals. Among those Hindu groups that practice vegetarianism, it is because of personal purity rather than a theological or philosophical respect for life. Meat is conceptually connected to gross materiality, while vegetables and in some instances fish are less compromised by the taint of embodiment. We see this in the vegetarian Greek Pythagoreans and also the thirteenth-century Christian heretical movement of the Cathars or Albigensians. There is some reason to doubt the real force or even the existence of this heresy, as opposed to the paranoid imaginings or opportunistic constructions of their persecutors, but even if largely invented, vegetarianism was regarded as a suspicious and even dangerous form of anti-materialism.

Far from disparaging meat or believing it weighs down the soul, the Abrahamic religions allow or even celebrate carnivorous eating. As in most religions, adepts and the unusually devout might give up meat, but because Judaism, Christianity, and Islam emphasize the essential goodness of Creation, it is considered inappropriate if not heretical to insist on a binary view of evil matter versus good spirit.

The Book of Genesis states that God considered what He had created to be good and this was interpreted to mean that meat-eating is natural and appropriate, at least after the Fall, and that abstaining from meat defies the essential virtue of matter and flesh. Attitudes vary from Islam, which praises meat-eating, to Catholic Christianity, which enjoins periodic abstinence. In one of the many collected sayings (Hadith) of the Prophet Mohammed, he is supposed to have said, "The lordliest food of the people of this world and of Paradise is meat." For Muslims and Jews, however, not all animals are licit. Both abhor pork, and Jews also prohibit consuming shellfish. Even approved animals must be slaughtered appropriately. Neither the blood nor the hindquarters can be used, and the process must be certified by religious authorities as halal or kosher.

Christianity, on the other hand, tolerates a wide range of meats and does not mandate how to kill animals. Early Christians criticized the Jews for adhering literally and stubbornly to old-law provisions rather than embracing the liberating spirit. The followers of the new religion, unconstrained by the detailed instructions of Leviticus and Deuteronomy, regarded themselves as omnivores. According to Christian apologists, Jewish dietary regulations were legalistic remnants of an Old Testament superseded by the religion of the heart brought by Christ to his followers. In actual practice, Christian Europe did come to regard certain things as interdicted, if not in formal religious terms, at least according to civilized custom. A dialogue from fourteenth-century Bruges, intended to teach French to Flemish children, lists a number of meats that one should not eat. From our standpoint, some animals from this list, such as horses or bulls, are merely unappealing. Elephant seems unlikely, while griffins do not in fact exist. Cats and dogs are real and everywhere at hand (unlike elephants), but to eat them was thought to be noxious and it still is. Nevertheless, as Saint Augustine observed, context is important in deciding about food. Locusts are not normally considered edible, yet John the Baptist lived off them in the desert wilderness, while Esau's perfectly ordinary pottage, for which he sold his birthright to his brother Jacob, was sinful.

However open Christianity was to a variety of foods, the religion was not based on earthly pleasure. Among worldly delights to be avoided was excessive delight in eating. Gluttony was one of the Seven Deadly Sins, along with pride, sloth, anger, envy, covetousness, and lust. As a personal failing, gluttony may seem out of place in this list, not a worthy rival to lust or greed. Yet in the present secular culture, overeating is probably more disparaged than any of the other formerly deadly sins, many of which, such as pride, are now considered virtues. The average affluent American spends more time worrying about gluttony-related matters such as diet, body-mass ratio, and nutrition than about a propensity to anger or covetousness.

Medieval analysis of gluttony went beyond just overeating. Pope Gregory the Great (died 604 A.D.) categorized gluttony to encompass eating too quickly, dining too frequently or irregularly, and displaying gastronomic connoisseurship. Desire for rare, delicate dishes or a passion for showy ingredients such as spices were as wicked as common greediness. Because gastronomic sophistication involves discussion of meals, comparisons, ratings, and critiques, the discourse of gourmandise is, in Catholic teaching, a dangerous distraction, involving as it does self-indulgence and showing off. By their very purpose, the Michelin guides and their imitators are, according to this tradition, sinful.

The condemnation of gluttony in Catholic Christianity does not mean disdain for food; quite the contrary, church teachings elevated food to a degree of sacred symbolism found in few other religions. The central ritual connecting the created world to the Divine is the Eucharist, in which bread and wine are transformed into the body and blood of Christ by the officiating priest. To varying degrees the Protestant versions have interpreted this ceremony as merely commemorative, but the Catholic understanding is that the elements of the Eucharist undergo transubstantiation at the moment of consecration. Catholicism also has a venerable tradition of extreme fasting by consuming only the unique sacred bread of the Eucharist. Symbolic food is compatible with self-mortification.

Sin, which plays a large role in the Christian outlook and psychology, is to be rectified by, among other things, a dietary regime dictated by the calendar, one that does not require heroic fasting but imposes some inconvenience at least. The cycle of abstinence in Catholic practice emphasizes the days of Advent before Christmas and the forty days of Lent before Easter. Renouncing certain kinds of food during these periods is a spiritual and expiatory experience. Catholic regulations before the Second Vatican Council of 1962–1965 were more complex than what is ordained by Yom Kippur, the single Jewish day of atonement, or the straightforward, if arduous, observance of Islamic Ramadan. Christian abstinence did not mean eating less, but rather giving up meat and other animal products.

Not surprisingly, carnality and its renunciation were most effectively symbolized by meat, which was prohibited during fasting days. Nevertheless, the regulations were not intended to deny all gustatory pleasure: spices and sugar, for example, were permitted during times of abstinence. In addition to Lent and Advent, certain days of the week required fasting. Friday was the most important, as it commemorates the Crucifixion, but in the Middle Ages some pastoral guides recommended that the pious and scrupulous abstain on Wednesday (the day that Judas received the money to betray Jesus) and Saturday (dedicated to Mary). Vigils of important saints' commemorations and other solemn occasions could also require fasts.

There were at least ninety yearly days of abstinence in European Christianity before the Reformation, and the Eastern Orthodox churches were (and remain) equally rigorous. According to one's degree of piety and to some extent the regulations of ecclesiastical dioceses, as many as two hundred days a year might require or at least recommend fasts. Lent was less negotiable, although toward the end of the Middle Ages dispensations to consume butter during this most serious penitential season were not uncommon. For meat, however, Lenten rules were quite inflexible, and apart from what was permitted to Jewish communities, butchering shut down entirely.

The rules of fasting influenced the dietary regime of the Christian Middle Ages, with the fishing industry the largest beneficiary. Meals on fast days centered on fish, the importance of which in medieval Europe can scarcely be exaggerated. Seafood that could be treated to preserve its otherwise extremely perishable character was particularly profitable. The trade in salted (white) and smoked (red) herring from the North and Baltic Seas was immense, as was the traffic in dried cod (stockfish) and salt cod (bacalao). For the wealthy, the variety of fish available meant that the most rigorous fasting season did not require giving up interesting and luxurious dishes. The household account books of an early fifteenth-century bishop of Salisbury in England mention forty-two different kinds of fish and shellfish.

The clergy, even monks who were required to follow a more limited diet than priests, were well known for their gourmandise. The skill of the chefs at the monastery of Cluny in preparing what was technically a cuisine of abstinence (vegetables, cereals, fish) was the target of the Cistercian Saint Bernard's attack on the scandalous luxury of the rival order of the Benedictine monks. In his *Apologia,* written in 1125 to counter accusations that he had slandered the Cluniacs, Bernard denounced their hypocritical regimen of austerity:

> Course after course is served and in the place of a single one of meat, which is abstained, there are two great courses of fish. And when you have been sated by the first, if you touch the second, it will seem that you have not even tasted fish yet. The reason is that they are all prepared with such care and skill by the cooks that, four or five courses having been devoured, the first does not impede the appetite.

Lay people of means were even less inclined than Benedictine monks to go hungry during days of abstinence. On a Friday in July 1483, during a cycle of banquets for the coronation of King Richard III of England, the fish (or what were considered fish) included salted lamprey, pike (as a soup), plaice in a "Saracen" sauce, sea crabs, fried gurnard, baked conger eel, grilled tench, bass in pastry, sole, salmon in pastry, perch in pastry, shrimp, trout, and roast porpoise.

As such dinners suggest, fasting in the medieval Christian tradition tended to become technical observance of specific food prohibitions without sacrificing quantity or quality. Protestant reformers, who abolished the fasting calendar, ridiculed Catholic dietary laws as legalistic and insincere. Fasting days evoked a strategic rather than pious response and afforded opportunities for corruption by paying church officials for exceptions. Martin Luther preached against the indulgences granted by the pope to raise funds for rebuilding St. Peter's basilica in the Vatican, and it was considered similarly scandalous that a new tower at the cathedral of Rouen was nicknamed the "butter tower" because its construction had been financed through an indulgence allowing—in return for a fee, of course—the consumption of butter during fasting intervals.

Laxity was not universal, however. The fourteenth and fifteenth centuries saw widely publicized cases of extreme fasting. Here holy food and self-mortification were combined, as saintly ascetic figures such as Saint Catherine of Siena (1347–1380) or Christina "the Astonishing" (1150–1224) lived on little more than the Eucharist. This was not merely an individual choice, for such women had followers and influenced the great world of politics. Catherine of Siena prevailed on the pope to move back to Rome after decades of residing in Avignon, a papal enclave in southern France. The result of what was at first a triumphant return to the apostolic city turned into the Great Schism, which lasted from 1378 to 1417.

For ordinary Catholics, the main hardship during times of abstinence was monotony rather than hunger. Luxuries such as dried fruit were permitted during Lent and consumed in large quantities. Traders rushed to supply northern Europe with Mediterranean and Middle Eastern dates, apricots, prunes, and the like. With the arrival of Easter, demand always dropped sharply as there was henceforth a normal variety of less expensive things available to eat. A fifteenth-century merchant of Bristol named Nicholas Palmer bought dried fruit in Andalucía to sell in England, but the ship was delayed by bad weather and arrived after Easter. Since it was no longer fasting season, he was unable to sell his cargo at a profit and the venture turned into a financial disaster.

The end of Lent was sometimes celebrated by rituals of contempt for fasting staples. Until not so long ago, on Maundy Thursday at the French town of St. Rémy a parade of clergy dragged roped red (smoked) herrings through the streets. This fatigue with herrings is understandable. The fish was inescapable during Lent, as can be seen from the menus of institutions such as schools, hospitals, and almshouses. At the well-funded leper-hospital of Grand-Beaulieu in Chartres, inmates normally received meat three times a week and soup four times for their principal meal. During Lent and Advent, however, they ate mostly herring, occasionally varied with some other salted fish. To mark vigils, they were allowed cheese and eggs.

Food's religious importance extends beyond fasting, as it also serves agendas of religious discrimination and persecution. The Spanish Inquisition's suspicions of *conversos*, Jewish converts to Christianity, centered around obdurate "Judaizing" practices such as not cooking on the Sabbath. There are no medieval Sephardic cookbooks in existence, but indirectly we know a lot about Spanish Jewish cuisine from Inquisitorial documents, especially for the period after the expulsion of 1492. After that date, no one in Spain any longer openly followed the Jewish religion, and the church devoted its investigative and prosecutorial attention to *conversos* suspected of secretly maintaining Jewish observances and ceremonies.

Inquisitorial sources are voluminous and well preserved. A complex bureaucracy, the Holy Office, as it was known, was meticulous in gathering and keeping records. It focused considerable attention on food, using paid informants and encouraging servants and neighbors to report suspicious habits. Itinerant inquisitorial panels arriving at a town would offer a grace period during which infractions could be reported voluntarily. Inhabitants were encouraged to come forward to confess their own trespasses and inform on their friends, neighbors, and employers in return for immunity or at least relaxation of the law's wrath.

Examples of what the church authorities considered Judaizing customs included cooking on Fridays the food to be eaten on the Jewish Sabbath; cleaning meat of blood and cutting away fat, nerves, and sinews from the leg of an animal; refusing to eat pork, rabbit, strangled birds, cuttlefish, eels, and other scaleless fish; dining on boiled eggs at funerals; consuming meat during Lent and other fasting times; and preparing special foods for Passover. Trials included testimony about the food practices of *conversos* who followed the rituals of their ancestral religion. The records do not give detailed recipes, but the inquisitors identify certain ingredients, dishes, and methods of preparation that were supposedly Jewish.

Eggplant, chickpeas, onions, garlic, and chard were eaten by everyone, but nevertheless typified as Jewish. Satiric poems called *cancioneros* made fun of Jews and *conversos* who still practiced Judaism. In the mid-fifteenth century, Rodrigo Cota wrote about the nuptials of the grandson of the *converso* finance minister to King Enrique IV of Castile to a young woman related to the eminent Cardinal Mendoza. He called the ceremony a Jewish wedding and noted that the groom consumed neither pork nor fish without scales. The presence of an eggplant casserole with saffron and chard, the poet implied, was suspicious.

Consuming specific foods would not by itself get you in trouble with the Inquisition, but it might indicate a pattern worth investigation. Unleavened bread during Passover was obviously compromising, as were koshering meat, avoiding pork, and failing to practice Christian fasting. The kitchen was the common scene of religious crimes. Non-Jewish servants testified about the cooking habits of *converso* families. Shortly after 1500, Maria Bernal of Almazan was accused by her servant Francisca of ordering that meat be trimmed of all fat and the veins picked out. The meat had to be "soaked in water five or six times until it was white and dead looking," the servant testified. In such cases the accused might offer the defense that this was simply what she did to keep meat from going bad in the summer, or that the culinary practices were devoid of religious significance. These exculpatory responses were seldom effective.

Equally common were allegations that Judaizing households prepared *adafina,* a stew cooked before the Sabbath began on Friday at sunset and kept covered in the oven near banked coals so that, even though no fire was lit, the dish would still be warm when consumed on Saturday afternoon. Inquisition records disclose numerous *adafina* recipes. A servant for a Toledo *converso* family reported that their household's Saturday meal consisted of chickpeas, meat, or udder, put into the pot with eggplant, dried coriander, caraway, cumin, pepper, and onion.

Another Sabbath dish was *almodrote de berenjena,* mashed eggplant prepared with cheese and eggs on Friday, and eaten cold on Saturday. Inquisitorial testimony also mentions eggplant fritters, baked omelets with vegetables (*fritadas*), and pies filled with ground meat. Sponge cake, almond cake, and quince paste (*membrillo*) were typical Sabbath desserts. Flourless cakes with almonds, eggs, and sugar, flavored with orange, were baked for Passover.

Shunning pork was so well known that it provided fodder for the satirical *cancioneros* introduced above. Although there are many instances in which *conversos* publicly ate pork, that too was deemed suspicious, a dramatic gesture to deflect attention from a host of everyday Judaizing practices, including avoidance of what was deemed "normal" pork consumption. The *conversos* of Majorca were known as *Xuetes* (*xua* meaning bacon in Majorcan Catalan), because their ancestors cooked and ate bacon in public to show their sincerity, but they only did this once or twice a year. It is worth noting that today in China's Xinjiang province, Muslim Uyghurs in internment camps are sometimes forced to eat pork as part of their "re-education."

Complementary with illicit observance of Judaism, *conversos* were accused of not adhering to Christian fasts, especially during Lent. A woman named Aldonza Lainez served laborers in her fields a turnip stew in Lent (no problem), but then ordered her servant to top it with grated cheese and laughed at the workers' startled reaction. A servant for a family in Toledo in 1621 said they secretly cooked meat during Lent, including, oddly enough, blood sausage. The family tried to hide this activity from the servants by sending them upstairs, but apparently this stratagem did not work.

Religious dietary prohibitions and practices are familiar to outsiders. In the contemporary West, non-Muslims are aware of the term "halal" even if they have no knowledge of any other Islamic teachings. In today's post-religious or at least non-observant settings—that is, most of Europe and much of North America— the language of religious abhorrence is applied to a discourse of secular morality with meat at its center. Abstaining from meat can be presented as a personal option, but it mobilizes a quasi-religious prescriptive force against those who refuse to acknowledge its virtue. Advocating a vegetable-based diet can be justified as an avoidance of cruelty to animals, advancing personal health, and relieving an unsustainable environmental burden. The third aspect in particular implies a demand on a larger public. In *Eating Animals,* the writer Jonathan Safran Foer, for example, urges the universal adoption of a vegan diet in order to prevent environmental catastrophe.

Adherence to vegetarianism, its stronger cousin veganism, or its more complaisant offshoot the "vegetable-forward" regimen expresses some of the same moral tone as religious law. It also serves as a vehicle of self-identification in which considerations of politics (blue versus red states) and gender (female versus male) overlap. Defenders of meat at first simply argue freedom of personal choice, as do those attempting to prevent regulating sugary drinks or mandating wearing masks during an epidemic. A more aggressive register is to accuse would-be reformers of an ideological agenda and to claim for meat a naturalistic vindication, that human beings were created as carnivores.

Finally, food traditions can reinforce an otherwise weakening religious identity. *Gastronomic Judaism,* the title of a book by Jonathan Brumberg-Kraus, refers not only to the dietary laws of kashrut but typifies a sentiment found among Jews whose religious observance has lapsed, but who still consider themselves Jewish because they eat pastrami or celebrate Passover with proper special dishes. Food provides a connection among immigrant generations, and although a cuisine can seldom be preserved intact under conditions of assimilation, it survives vestigially as a symbolic language, especially at holidays. Orthodox Jews have not wavered in upholding the dietary laws, but elsewhere, as the tide of religious ritual recedes, food becomes a repository not of law or ceremony but of an acculturated sense of identity. Food is still important for memory and culture, but not as a sacred practice.

3 taste

The starting point for European expansion had nothing to do with the rise of any religion or the rise of capitalism—but it had a great deal to do with pepper.

—HENRY HOBHOUSE

Taste—what people like to eat as opposed to the biological sense—is a matter of individual preference. You may like asparagus, but I do not. Taste also is a real or imagined group cultural fact: Americans on average are fond of sugar and sweet dishes, a trait not shared, at least not until recently, by people in China. Even in our relatively homogeneous world, travel brings these contrasting preferences into relief with sometimes shockingly hot food or the ubiquity of organ meat. Here we look at how new tastes and culinary innovations have been motives for historical change, often violently destroying existing cultures and creating new ones.

Historically certain products with exotic tastes have been sought, especially when they were not capable of being locally cultivated. The elite of the Roman Empire were so enchanted with what was apparently a sharp, aromatic flavor of an herb called silphium, found in what is now Libya, that it was extinct by the end of the first century A.D. Infatuation with exotic imports may be frivolous in the sense that the product is unnecessary, but the passion among Europeans for such non-native commodities as spices and sugar had important, even cataclysmic historical consequences.

Frivolity may seem too strong a term for food that is optional, but it effectively conveys the paradox that the appetite for luxury goods has repeatedly caused historical shifts. Fashion and seemingly trivial, even silly new flavor sensations were motives for the European conquest and colonization that started in the sixteenth century. Pepper and other spices are hardly essential in the way that wheat or rice are, but they were desired with sufficient passion and traded for a high enough price to make it worthwhile to launch voyages to find them and so bypass intermediaries. The nearly simultaneous arrivals of the Portuguese adventurer da Gama in India and the Genoese servant of Spain Columbus in what he *thought* was India were the results of a quest to find the home of aromatic luxuries. One of da Gama's crew, asked ruefully by a North African Muslim trader, "What ill wind drew you here?" responded, "We have come for Christians and spices."

The medieval spice trade, a matter of supply, has received more attention than have questions relating to the demand that drove it, particularly why spices were so attractive in the first place. An enduring but wrong answer is that they were needed to preserve meat or to cover up the taste of spoiled food. The availability of cheaper and more effective methods of preservation such as smoking, salting, drying, and pickling renders this idea groundless. Spices were alluring because of their attributed medicinal value, their mysterious origins and high cost, but at the heart of their appeal was their flavor. Spices are required in three-quarters of the recipes from the approximately 150 surviving medieval cookbooks, and in considerably greater quantity and variety than is implied by a modern instruction such as "add pepper" or "serve with grated nutmeg."

The medieval preference for piquant flavor was not the preserve of the aristocracy. A commodity that few can afford will not have global economic impact. Today, extraordinary luxuries—wines such as Montrachet or Romanée Conti that cost thousands of dollars per bottle—are not widely marketed or even widely known. The way to make real money is through a scalable luxury, something most people can pay for if they want it. In the Middle Ages, the better-off clergy, urban merchants, and eventually even the upper levels of the peasantry bought spices, inclining more to pepper and ginger at the lower end of the price spectrum than really expensive ones such as cloves or nutmeg. To the best of their ability, the merely prosperous imitated princely and noble dining, and spices became the mark of comfort and good living for a large enough number of people to make the spice trade worthwhile.

The medieval practice of putting spices in everything was not perpetuated by modern European cuisines. After about 1700, spices were generally exiled to desserts—no more cinnamon sprinkled on pasta or fish. By contrast, enthusiasm for sugar grew exponentially. For England, per capita annual consumption of sugar was four pounds at the beginning of the eighteenth century, eighteen pounds at the beginning of the nineteenth century, and sixty pounds at the beginning of the twentieth. It is now over 150 pounds per year. Sugar is not a biological necessity any more than spices are. From Han Dynasty China to the Roman Empire, great civilizations managed perfectly well without it, relying on honey, which is less sweet than sugar and not as versatile because of its own particular taste.

It would be hard to come up with another edible commodity that equals sugar for disastrous historical impact. Transforming the Caribbean islands and Brazil into sugar cane plantations and processing centers was realized through the African slave trade, a labor recruitment system of unmatched brutality. According to James Fox, a vigorous opponent of slavery writing in 1791, every cup of tea or any other beverage sweetened with sugar is "steeped in the blood of our fellow creatures." The itinerant protagonist of Voltaire's *Candide* seeks information from a black slave in the West Indies who is stretched out on the ground, missing a hand and a leg. The unfortunate man tells the relentlessly optimistic youth that having lost a finger in the sugar refining machinery, his whole hand was cut off as a punishment for his carelessness. His attempt to run away was punished by having a leg amputated: "This is the price that must be paid so that you can eat sugar in Europe." Lest this seem a gruesome philosophical fiction, Orlando Patterson's recent account of Jamaica, *The Confounding Island,* describes equally atrocious incidents from the era of slavery.

European demand created immense profits for sugar cultivation, refining, shipping, and distribution despite logistical, not to say moral, difficulties. The great surge in consumption began when sugar was added to three newly fashionable caffeinated beverages: tea, coffee, and chocolate. None of these had required sugar when they were first developed. The Chinese to this day do not serve sugar with tea; coffee in Arabia was not originally sweetened; the Mesoamerican elite drank chocolate with hot peppers, flowers, and other aromatic flavorings. The vagaries of taste led Europeans to prefer sweet, hot beverages, preferably accompanied by sugary pastries, cookies, and biscuits. In eighteenth-century Spain, already sweetened hot chocolate almost required an accompaniment of *melindros* (long biscuits with a spongy texture) that later gave way to *churros* (long strips of fried dough rolled in sugar). The European predilection for sugar moved people around the world, for the most part catastrophically.

Tea, coffee, and chocolate have different histories and sociologies. Coffeehouses created new forms of association in London after 1650. Convivial but less inebriating than taverns, they served as clearing houses for news and ideas. The first stock exchange, Lloyds (the first modern insurance partnership), and the Royal Academy (a scientific society) were all born in London coffeehouses.

Tea became popular in Britain at the end of the seventeenth century. Presented in a more domestic setting than coffee was, tea began its European career as a facilitator of upper-class sociability, especially among women. Tea was served using fine utensils made of silver and porcelain, accompanied by rituals involving the addition of milk, hot water, and sugar. By the nineteenth century, tea had become a democratic beverage particularly in Britain, consumed in great quantities by industrial workers as well as aristocrats, but signs of class difference persisted. To this day, members of the British upper orders add milk to poured-out tea, while what is left of the traditional working class puts the milk in the cup first and then adds the tea.

Chocolate, originally a New World product, preceded coffee and tea in popularity. By 1600, chocolate imported from its American empire was in vogue in Spain. At first, the chocolate served among the fashionable elite of Seville or Madrid was near-ly the same as what the indigenous people of Mexico drank, with spicy or herbal flavors, but no sugar. Adding sugar was a crucial innovation, and in the seventeenth century chocolate spread all over Europe as a hot, sweet beverage. White's, perhaps the most prestigious private club in London, first did business in 1693 as a hot-chocolate establishment. Later chocolate lost ground among sophisticates and became identified with women and children. Hot chocolate did retain its status in southern Europe, particu-larly Spain, but as with chocolate candy, it became a feminized treat more than a daily necessity like coffee or tea.

The desire for exotic products fueled the consolidation of colo-nial empires and helped make imperial projects profitable. A study of consumption patterns shows that in 1559, the proportion of overseas, non-European goods to all edible goods sold was less than ten percent; by 1800 it was thirty-five percent. Sugar, tea, chocolate, and coffee were much less expensive than they had been in the seventeenth century, but the profits merchants and manufacturers might have lost in unit value were more than made up in sales volume.

There is currently nothing that equals the influence that caf-feinated beverages and sugar had on labor and production in the seventeenth and eighteenth centuries. Or maybe because so much is global now, no individual commodity or new fashion stands out. Kiwi fruit modestly affected eating habits in the 1980s, and Italy now outproduces New Zealand, the nation after whose avi-an mascot the fruit was originally named, but kiwi has not dra-matically reshaped the contemporary scene. Bananas have had a greater impact. No biological impetus requires eating bananas for breakfast, and they do not grow in the countries that consume them the most. Bananas' transformative impact can be read in the history of Central America, the colonial-like power once enjoyed there by the United Fruit Company, and the opprobrious term "banana republic," used contemptuously to label poorly governed states and then appropriated as a brand for a chain of clothing stores. As with chocolate, tea, and coffee, the trajectory of bananas is from luxury to quotidian, to the point where they are taken for granted and no longer perceived as exotic.

Today's food preferences show a number of paradoxes. The Solomon Islands have the largest per capita consumption of sweet potatoes in the world; more tomatoes are eaten proportionately in Libya and the United Arab Emirates than in Italy. Phenomena of this sort do not, however, alter society. Nevertheless, the prestige, alleged health value, and sheer novelty of certain foods have had recent unfortunate consequence. The coronavirus epidemic may have started as a disease in bats, transmitted to humans by eating them or other exotic creatures they infected—a contemporary example of the power of prejudicial notions of what "other people" eat, the Chinese in this case becoming objects of fear and disdain as their culinary tastes were deemed responsible for the epidemic.

If no single food fashion has remade the contemporary world, the cumulative indirect consequences of globalization have been fateful, sometimes comical, and often bad. Quinoa was an unremarked staple of the Andean regions, but around 2010, it was taken up in North America as miraculously healthful. The quinoa industry proclaimed 2013 as "the year of quinoa," by which time quinoa had become too expensive for many Peruvians, who had previously subsisted on it, to afford. World demand meant that well-capitalized Peruvian farmers could make money, but the crop was now too valuable to sell to the domestic market.

The reverse, adopting something never eaten before, happened in the sub-Saharan nation of Burkina Faso, which supplies a considerable proportion of the string beans eaten in France, its former colonial ruler. It is not that the country's climate and soil are especially suited for string beans, any more than Mexico is perfect for asparagus; the logic is related to the relative cheapness of land and labor. The *haricots verts* are shipped by air out of the capital city, Ouagadougou. French buyers refuse to accept beans with imperfections in appearance (not bright green) or texture (too soft), and so some crates do not make the flight. The beans left behind are unexceptionable to an impoverished local population. Because of the plethora of rejects, string beans, previously unknown in Burkina Faso, have become a substantial part of the diet.

Of more cumulative significance than these anomalies is the devastation wrought on the world's forests and climate by palm oil, which may be, in fact, the sugar of our times. Once heralded as a godsend, palm oil is free of trans fats and cheap to grow, as the trees are extremely productive. Palm oil is so versatile that it is an ingredient in around fifty percent of all items on supermarket shelves, ranging from cosmetics to ice cream, from frozen pizzas to toothpaste. Thirty-eight percent of world vegetable oil production is from palms and eighty percent of it comes from Indonesia and Malaysia, where its cultivation has annihilated forests and uprooted villages. Former forest lands cleared of native trees are then planted with thousands of palms in rows. Burning tropical forests accounts for at least one-tenth of all human-generated carbon dioxide emissions, and as the jungles of Kalimantan (Borneo) and Sumatra have been decimated, orangutans and about two hundred other animal and plant species are in danger of extinction, and humans too have had to move away. The palm trees require large quantities of artificial fertilizer and pesticides, which the prevailing rainy climate causes to run off into rivers, polluting whatever cultivable land survives.

The impact of this rapacious form of agriculture is not a secret. As with many sectors of the corporate food world, the palm oil industry tries to present itself as moving toward sustainability now that it is unable simply to deny the facts. Global communications and satellite photography show the damage, and there is plenty of agitation about the situation. Eloquent but ineffectual denunciation of the depravity of power and the suffering of ordinary people is not new. Bartolomé de las Casas demonstrated the disastrous effects of Spanish colonization on the original inhabitants of the New World in his *Short Description of the Destruction of the Indies* (1552), and this bestseller produced a considerable amount of hand-wringing. The American natives continued to be enslaved and die, however.

4 rejecting and enjoying the food of others

Chicken Tikka Massala is now a true British national dish, not only because it is the most popular, but because it is a perfect illustration of the way Britain absorbs and adapts external influences.

—BRITISH FOREIGN SECRETARY ROBIN COOK, APRIL 19, 2001

A common way of describing and defining barbarians is to make up stories about their eating customs. The Greeks portrayed the Scythians as nomadic predators who spoke an incomprehensible jabber. Frighteningly tough, they appeared to be indifferent to comfort. A widespread idea about savage people was that they ate raw or inadequately cooked food. Ammianus Marcellinus (ca. 330–400), the leading chronicler of the late Roman Empire, wrote that the Huns uncomplainingly endured hunger, cold, and thirst, rendering them all the fiercer and more militarily effective. What need did they have for savory food? They happily subsisted on roots of wild plants and "the half-raw flesh of any kind of animal whatever, which they put between their thighs and the backs of their horses, thus warming it a little." The story has had recurrent appeal as a vivid symbol of toughness. Accounts of the Mongol invasions of the thirteenth century revived the same image of relentless nomads making do with meat heated by sweaty horses. The master of gastronomic belles-lettres Jean Anthelme Brillat-Savarin quotes a Croatian military captain telling him in 1815 about the same method of on-the-go meat preparation.

"Steak tartare," invented in late-nineteenth-century Europe, takes its name from the recollection of attributed nomadic tastes.

The image of the barbarian begins as the opposite of civilization but can end up being fashionable and slightly comic. No one really thinks that Tartars routinely ate finely chopped raw beef with beaten eggs, onions, capers, and ground pepper any more than they really believe hearty, "rustic" dishes reproduce what peasants actually ate. Nevertheless, other people's food can be a mark of their unpleasant strangeness and yet, simultaneously, something to be imitated and adopted by those who see themselves as civilized and superior.

Appalling peoples outside the perceived perimeters of civilization were not the only recipients of culinary contempt. The persistent association of the French with frogs, or the derisive nickname "Kraut" for a German are examples of the casual dismissal of the food of economically advanced but nevertheless occasionally despised foreigners. Even more common, however, is the use of food to disparage the familiar lower orders within the same society. The food of the impoverished majority has often been ridiculed by their social superiors.

Medieval writers made fun of the food habits of the peasantry. Opinion in the Middle Ages was divided as to whether peasants actually *liked* lowly and unpleasant fare such as gruel or root vegetables, or would eat better food given the opportunity, in which latter case their regimen was a sign of involuntary subjugation. Authors of satires portrayed the peasant as happy with his lot and unsuited for anything better. A French story (*fabliau*) of the thirteenth century features a well-off peasant who marries into a socially superior bourgeois family. His wife prepares the moderately elegant food she grew up with, but her husband finds that its complexity and subtlety do not agree with him and he suffers from indigestion. The peasant recovers quickly once his wife starts fixing humble dishes for him like peas soaked in milk. In another *fabliau,* a rustic driving a cart of manure through the streets of Montpellier faints, overcome by the unfamiliar fragrance from the town's famous spice market. The cart is blocking traffic and efforts to revive the peasant are unsuccessful until a clever bystander puts a pellet of manure under his nose, whereupon, refreshed by the aroma of home, he is restored to health.

In the modern world too, the poor are reputed to eat unhealthful and unpleasant food, often of dubious wild origins, whether it is the "bush" food of Africa or opossum, raccoon, or squirrel in Appalachia. Gastronomic opprobrium attaches even more to ethnicity than class. Toward the end of the nineteenth century, African Americans were mocked in all manner of satiric literature, music, and theatrical performances. They were depicted as fond of food that white people (allegedly) would not have any part of, such as chitterlings or hog's maw, or comically rapturous about "normal" items such as fried chicken or watermelon.

The ambiguities of culinary admiration and marginalization are particularly apparent as applied to immigrants. Restaurants will be discussed in a later chapter on conviviality, but here it is worth citing some examples of foreign cuisines adapted to American tastes showing the paradoxes of welcome and mistrust, of opportunity and discrimination that greet unfamiliar food. No foreign cuisine was more successful in the United States than that of the Chinese immigrants who began to arrive shortly after word of the California Gold Rush traveled across the globe in 1849.

Adapted to American tastes, the cooking of the south China coast, especially the Pearl River Delta region in Guangdong, proved popular with so-called Bohemians, urban sophisticates who liked experimentation and possessed some discretionary income. Comfortably unconventional, these journalists, lawyers, and other arty if not actually artistic people were the ancestors of Yuppies and Hipsters, tastemakers who over the past fifty years have made up a large segment of the restaurant-going public.

The popularity of Chinese food (or what purported to be Chinese food) accelerated during what was dubbed the "Chop Suey Craze" that started in 1897 with the visit of a Chinese government official to the United States. The emissary's chef, it was widely if inaccurately reported, prepared this novel dish at the Waldorf Hotel in New York City. By 1910, there were hundreds of chop suey restaurants in New York patronized by all types of people, not just adventurous Bohemians. Other immigrant groups too were enchanted with Chinese restaurants. An 1890 article in the magazine *American Hebrew* expressed bewilderment at the Jewish predilection for manifestly unkosher Chinese food, and in 1928 the Yiddish newspaper *Der Tag* published "Di Milkhkhome tsvishn Tshap-sui un Gefilte Fish" (The War Between Chop Suey and Gefilte Fish).

Widespread affection for Chinese food did nothing to remedy the deteriorating situation of the Chinese in the United States. Aspiring Chinese immigrants were the first to be singled out for state-sponsored discrimination when the unambiguously titled Chinese Exclusion Act of 1882 forbade anyone of Chinese origin except merchants and students from entering the United States. Although there were ways of evading the full force of this and successive legislation, by 1900 the rate of Chinese immigration had fallen by more than eighty percent. Formally and informally, the Chinese already in the country were shut out of jobs such as railroad and agricultural work that they had previously been heavily involved in. The fact that in disproportionate numbers Chinese Americans were restaurant and laundry workers and owners of such businesses was because these enterprises were exceptions to the discrimination, not because of innate talent or inclination.

Indian curry restaurants in Britain have been similarly the objects of simultaneous affection and disdain. Among the most devoted frequenters of curry houses were working-class men looking for spicy food to soak up the beer after the pubs closed. The customer might forget whether he had ordered the murgh masala or the murgh korma—and still did not know when the food arrived—but it went down well, especially given its low price. The contempt for Indian cuisine and Indian people implicit in this outlook is evoked in Martin Amis's novel *London Fields* from 1989. The small-time criminal Keith Talent eats regularly at Indian restaurants, including "Amritsar" and "The Indian Mutiny." At the latter he challenges the kitchen to make a mutton vindaloo that is hot enough for his satisfaction (with "napalm sauce"). Insular and bigoted, Keith nevertheless considers eating curry to be as typical of being British as playing darts and drinking beer.

Some of the same mixture of culinary admiration and scorn is often applied in the United States to Mexican immigrants. It is not only possible but common to hold the opinion that Mexicans illegally crossing the border represent a threat and simultaneously to patronize Mexican restaurants. The conceit that cross-cultural dining experience builds tolerance and understanding is an illusion marketed by the tourism industry.

Of course, ways of thinking about foreign food can change. The case of Japanese sushi in the United States is archetypal. Inexpensive Japanese restaurants experienced a modest success in the early twentieth century, selling Westernized dishes such as tempura and sukiyaki. It was well known that authentic Japanese food involved raw fish, but culinary observers assumed that it was impossible for non-Japanese to imitate this predilection. A *Los Angeles Times* writer in 1934 stated that local "Nipponese" restaurants were popular, but that white Angelenos stayed away from sushi and sashimi, their clear favorite being sukiyaki.

Only in the late 1960s did this change with the opening of the first sushi restaurants catering to non-Japanese customers, their success encouraged by the invention of the California roll, a starter-sushi without raw fish. By the 1990s, sushi was not only accepted, it was the object of a craze dwarfing even the chop suey madness of a century earlier. Teenagers, not noted at the time for their culinary adventurism, became particularly fond of this flavorful, fun, and seemingly nonfattening treat.

Ethnic restaurants prospered in the United States because of their inexpensive exoticism and the accommodations proprietors made to American tastes, leaving out dishes popular at home such as tripe that would not appeal to American patrons, moderating the spice content or making dishes sweeter. So-called ethnic restaurants became objects of affection but of a patronizing sort, the restaurant goer acting as critic, connoisseur, and judge of authenticity. Reviewers in newspapers, magazines, and later on websites such as Yelp congratulated themselves as food adventurers adept at discovering unspoiled locales.

The exception to this attitude was the French restaurant. In this case "foreign" does not carry the overtones of "ethnic." Until the 1980s, French restaurants were set apart because beginning around 1700 France defined international haute cuisine. The invention of the restaurant in its modern form took place in Paris in the 1770s. Until the late twentieth century, the authority of French culinary taste was recognized throughout the world. The Maison Dorée was the fanciest place to dine in Mexico City around 1900. In that year Delmonico's and Sherry's, rival French restaurants, battled for primacy in New York, and Moscow society dined at the impeccably French Hermitage restaurant. A meal served in 1910 at the grand Hotel des Indes in Batavia, Netherlands East Indies (now Jakarta, Indonesia), reveals no concession to the cuisine or climate of Java: *Consommé Montmorency* (clear chicken soup with asparagus tips and chicken quenelles); *Filet de boeuf garni à la Châtelaine* (beef filet with Madeira sauce, garnished with artichoke bottoms filled with soubise sauce, chestnuts, and noisette potatoes); *Filet de soles à l'Amiral* (poached sole with mushrooms, truffles, and a sauce made with butter and shrimp); and *Escalopes de ris de veau à la Villeroy* (cold braised sweetbreads with truffles and a ham and mushroom sauce).

Foreign food, therefore, can have considerable prestige, and that of France is not the only example. In classical Greece, the cuisines of Persia and Sicily were renowned for their exquisite and luxurious inventiveness. During the Middle Ages, European recipes imitated high-end Islamic food of the Middle East. Muslims might be infidels in the eyes of the Christian Europeans, but their upper classes enjoyed an enviable lifestyle, so it was fashionable to reproduce Islamic culinary tastes for perfumed food, dried fruit, rice, rosewater, and spice combinations. In our time, American fast food has been successful even in countries whose inhabitants detest the United States.

The hierarchy of culinary fashion has not been completely stable, and certain cuisines have been able to rise in prestige. While maintaining an inexpensive segment, Italian and Japanese restaurants have profited from the decline of French hegemony. For much of the twentieth century, these were in the same category as Chinese—cheap and colorful, offering standard items such as spaghetti and meatballs or yakitori. Now some of the most expensive restaurants are Japanese or Italian. This has been accomplished through images of Italy and Japan as fashion arbiters and the effective marketing of regional and authentic food. Americans now consider themselves well-informed about northern Italian or Tuscan cuisine and different Japanese service styles such as *kaiseki* (a formal order of courses dictated by season, region, and tradition) versus *omakase* (more spontaneous, leaving it to the chef to select).

Replicating and admiring the food of others, even scorned others, has a long history. A regular item at medieval feasts was *frumenty,* a peasant porridge of grain, milk, and egg. Meat, especially venison and other game, was added to make the aristocratic version. One English recipe collection in a manuscript known as the *Wagstaff Miscellany* has instructions for preparing frumenty with porpoise, an appropriate Lenten suggestion because porpoise was considered a fish.

Dressing up the food of the common people is a persistent theme. Today the once plebeian hamburger and pizza have been elevated to gourmet status. Sometimes this effect is achieved, as with the medieval frumenty, by adding a luxury ingredient, such as Daniel Boulud's burger made with foie gras. More commonly, the difference between the fast-food and high-end version is the quality of the meat as well as the fancier setting.

Patriotic solidarity can be expressed by exalting the dishes of the populace against foreign ways. By the eighteenth century, the beefsteak in Britain was put forward to oppose the "mucky sauces" and effeminate "kickshaws" (derived from *quelque chose,* "something or other") of the French. American presidential candidates from William Henry Harrison to George W. Bush used the supposed French tastes of their opponents to signal effeminate snobbery as opposed to a simple, masculine fondness for raw beef (Harrison) or, as mentioned earlier, pork rinds in the case of Bush the elder.

Such ridiculous assertions must be effective since both Harrison and Bush won; the gastronomic reality right now, however, favors not fervid "country-first" dining but rather the global growth of eclecticism. Whatever claims are made for polenta, pork rinds, pelmeni, or even chicken tikka masala in terms of national solidarity, the cities of the world have come to resemble each other in offering tacos, panini, sushi, pizza, and the like. At the close of the twentieth century, the main fear was the McDonaldization of the world. This has not quite happened. Beyond fast food, the United States is the transmission agent, not the inventor, for diverse and mixed-up dining practices. Sushi is originally Japanese, tacos Mexican, and pizza Italian, but their export and diffusion is via American heterogeneity. The food of others has become selectively accepted and globally marketed. It should be obvious that global eclecticism does not mean the growth of tolerance and cultural understanding.

An incident in the early spring of 2020 weaves together some strands followed in this chapter. The *New York Times* food columnist Alison Roman attracted unfavorable social media attention when she criticized organizing guru Marie Kondo and model Chrissy Teigen for self-aggrandizing marketing of their product lines. This seemed hypocritical because Roman was busy creating her own lifestyle image and even selling accessories to imitate it. She apologized for gratuitously attacking the two other women, one of whom is Asian, the other Asian American.

This was not the end of the affair, however, as Roman's whole approach was reexamined and attacked for culinary appropriation or, as Roxana Hadadi, a reviewer of movies and other media, put it, "colonialism as cuisine." Roman had curated her brand on the basis of eclectic simplicity, gentrifying the cuisine of black and brown people for a Caucasian audience. Roman marketed "easy" at the expense of culture, commenting on one of her recipes calling for canned chickpeas, coconut milk, ginger, and turmeric in these terms: "I'm like y'all, this is not a curry. I've never made a curry. I don't come from a culture that knows about curry. I come from no culture. I have no culture." Self-deprecating at first glance, the statement positions Roman as superior to all those cute foreign cuisines out there from which she has the privilege to pick and choose. By posting her recipes everywhere on social media, she profitably annexes culture to convenience, making no claims that her recipes lovingly reproduce the hard work of peasant or ethnic culinary traditions. What makes this different from garnishing medieval frumenty with venison is that what renders formerly rustic dishes worthy of elite attention is not expensive ingredients but rather no-fuss preparation. Consistent over time, however, is a dynamic of patronizing appropriation.

5 food and health

A man that lives on pork, fine-flour bread, rich pies and cakes and condiments, drinks tea and coffee and uses tobacco, might as well try to fly as be chaste in thought.

—JOHN HARVEY KELLOGG

I t is not necessary to underline the significance of food to health. Everyone recognizes that illness is related to poor diet, that even the affluent (and sometimes *especially* the affluent) make erroneous food choices, and that wellness is maintained or improved by attention to what one eats. Our society frames the relationship between food and health in terms of a science of nutrition, so that in theory, there should be agreed-upon evidence for beneficial versus harmful diets. That this does not work in practice can be seen by the simultaneous obsessive concern with dieting in the United States and the nation's high rate of obesity. It is not just that the scientists have changed their minds about what is or is not healthful—eggs have played both a villainous and a heroic role—but that even when dietary advice is clear and consistent, it doesn't align with what people like to eat, or with what is being advertised or what is cheap and readily available.

Teachings about diet, health, and illness are often framed in terms of equilibrium. A sensible diet will include complementary foods whose interactive effect is to balance proteins versus carbohydrates, or regulate sugar and salt, or not depend too much on meat. The notion of balance is of ancient and enduring attraction.

Ayurvedic medicine in India, traditional Chinese advice about avoiding illness, and classical Greek notions about internal fluids (humors) all center on achieving bodily equilibrium. Climate, astrology, wind, water, and directional orientation, but always and importantly food, have been thought to influence health. Every individual has what in pre-modern Western medicine was referred to as a particular temperament: biological traits that seldom are in perfect balance. The point of a dietary regimen is to allow for such bias and to correct it—thus one who is constituted with too much moisture should adjust by eating things that have drying effects. Diet is a form of health maintenance and preventive medicine, as well as a treatment for disease, one of whose main causes is disequilibrium among external and internal agents. The medical treatises attributed to Hippocrates (ca. 460–370 B.C.) and their refinement by the Greco-Roman physician Galen (ca. 130–199 A.D.) are the foundations for a classical tradition handed over to medieval Europe through Latin translation of Arabic translations from the Greek, along with the theories of Arab medical observers. A synthesis of Greek and Arab teachings dominated European medicine until the late eighteenth century.

Hippocratic theory starts with the seasons of the year. These affect bodily equilibrium, so that what you should eat is related to what will counteract seasonal imbalance. The Hippocratic *Aphorisms* identify seasonal transition, a form of natural disequilibrium, as a leading cause of illness: "It is chiefly the changes of the season that produce diseases." The Hippocratic Corpus, especially the treatise known as *Regimen in Health,* recommends dietary plans that follow the course of the year. Winter, for example, makes us cold and hard. It is best, therefore, to balance this by consuming warming, drying, and astringent dishes so as to heat up the body. Meat should be roasted in winter because of that method's drying effect rather than cooked by boiling, which humidifies.

Galen systematized Hippocratic discussions of diet, temperament, and nature, elaborating on the qualities and characteristics of the four bodily humors—yellow bile, blood, black bile, and phlegm—whose equilibrium determines health and disease. These fluids correspond to the four elements (fire, air, earth, and water), producing permutations of moist/dry, hot/cold that vary with the seasons. Spring sees the ascendency of the humor of blood and the element of air, producing heat and moisture. Summer is governed by yellow bile and fire, hot and dry elements. Autumn, black bile, and earth are all cold and dry, while winter, phlegm, and water are cold and moist. This gives a rather static picture, however, of what Galen envisaged as a shifting and dynamic system, for the individual humoral profile is affected by age, constitution, diet, stress, exercise, insomnia, and other factors besides time of the year. The unhealthful imbalance of humors can be offset by diet.

The transition from classical to medieval medical knowledge in the West was influenced by the reception of Arabic texts that elaborated on Greek sources and gave advice about the seasons and humoral effects, but with little specific dietary advice. To maintain humoral balance the pseudo-Aristotelian Arabic "Secret of Secrets," widely diffused in Latin translation, recommended chicken, quail, eggs, and wild lettuce in the spring and in summer veal, stewed chicken, and vinegary and bitter preparations.

The humoral theory of pathology faded and finally ended by the nineteenth century, superseded by advances in physiology and epidemiology, such as the elaboration of blood circulation by William Harvey, the discovery of bacteria by Henri Pasteur, and the realization that tainted water causes cholera and mosquitos transmit yellow fever and malaria. Modern scientific medicine has not, however, eliminated popular ideas of equilibrium; it has merely replaced them using new language. When people speak of detoxifying or avoiding gluten, they are not only seeking to prevent illness but to promote wellness, a state of positive well-being, not simply the absence of disease. The concept of wellness is a reification of older notions of equilibrium linking emotional outlook with the body. Food, extolled as a facilitator of well-being, is also denounced as a source of dangerous temptation.

Affluent individuals have always sought the advice of doctors but followed their counsel selectively. Because medical guidance often includes irksome prohibitions, it is hard to embrace consistently. Sometimes this difficulty is framed ruefully or humorously: that nothing eaten on vacation makes you gain weight, or that chocolate is exempt from diet rules. Many invoke an offset model: I have been eating healthful vegetable dishes for the past two days, so now I can order steak with Béarnaise sauce. Consciously or not, most people in the developed world follow thought patterns about health established long ago.

Modern dietary experts, especially but not exclusively in the United States, have maintained the ancient idea of bodily equilibrium and its link to spiritual well-being, but with a more punitive, less harmonious tinge. Since the rise of nutritional science, beginning in the late nineteenth century, balance has yielded to harsh self-control and renunciation. In medieval Europe, lamprey was considered dangerously cold and moist in humoral terms, but its threat could be reduced by accompanying it with black pepper sauce since the spice was hot and dry. For modern nutritionists, however, certain things are simply bad for you.

Body image ideals too are enforced by self-regulation. There is no such thing in contemporary Western cultures as "pleasingly plump," and although the expectations are more demanding for women than for men, obesity is held in general disdain. The purpose of modern fasting is not to alleviate sin or to approach God but rather to cultivate an improved self. The self is no longer nurtured by intellectual pondering or prayer but by physical abstinence and self-mortification (diet and exercise). The aphorism "Know thyself," inscribed at the entrance court of the Oracle of Delphi, meant a form of soul-searching. It has been replaced by "Improve thyself," a profoundly American secular and individual concept popularized by Ralph Waldo Emerson. His essay "Self-Reliance" from 1841 may be more influential than any other American text ever written. It seems appropriate if ironic that a magazine called *Self* is not about philosophy but exercise.

Self-improvement comes in several forms, from learning a new language to getting better at golf, but what we are concerned with is its ascetic, dietary nutritionism. The cult of nutritionism began in the late nineteenth century. It means a supposedly scientific set of dietary rules irrespective of pleasure or quality, reducing food to a set of nutrients. The "nutricentric personality," as Gyorgy Scrinis has termed it, takes no pleasure in food but is obsessed with its beneficial or harmful composition. Nutritionism claims scientific status because it breaks with the earlier assumption that the individual knows what is good for them. The content of nutritionists' advice has changed. In the early twentieth century ideas that have since been discredited held sway, such as that vegetables provide little to no nutritional benefit compared with meat, or that over-spiced food encourages alcoholism. What has not changed is the notion that food is full of dangers and opportunities. Expert guidance is needed to determine a winning diet, defined as one that makes you feel better and look better, not just one that is naturally healthful.

In the early twentieth century, that positive rather than fearmongering variety of nutritionism focused on retrofitting degraded products with lab-developed nutrients. For example, vitamins and minerals were added to highly processed bread, and vitamin C supplemented artificial fruit products. As it turns out, however, the body's absorption of these supposedly healthful additives is inferior to when they are present naturally. More characteristic of current nutritionism is taking charge of your weight and assuming responsibility for your own health. Self-actualization makes diet not just a prudent measure to guard against illness but a personal statement, conforming to what a successful person should look like and be like. Self-realization and self-control are combined into a form of expression and an austere kind of self-surveillance.

The origins of nutritionism are at the opening of the twentieth century, by which time immense advances had been marked in understanding biochemistry and physiology, such as the discovery of vitamins or the different functions of fats, carbohydrates, and proteins. These findings were in a way unsettling, because no longer was eating what you like a functional guide to good health. Unseen and untasted factors had great influence, so that, for example, lack of vitamin C turned out to be the cause of scurvy. At different times invisible chemicals, from carbohydrates to preservatives, have been identified as dangerous while others such as vitamins or antioxidants are considered miraculously healthful.

Just as there were invisible healthful and perilous ingredients, there must be practices such as exercise or meditation that would dramatically improve not only bodily health but mental condition as well. A nostrum of the early twentieth century was what was called "Fletcherizing," named after a wealthy scientific popularizer named Horace Fletcher, who touted the virtues of chewing food thoroughly, one hundred times at least, before swallowing. He received support from scientists, particularly the chemist Russell Chittenden at Yale University. Fletcher's followers, including luminaries such as Henry James, claimed that adopting this regime not only relieved digestive problems but brought about psychological benefits, such as greater optimism and better mental focus. This is vintage nutritionism in the sense that what the food tastes like does not matter. Even if it is unpleasant, a supposedly scientific regimen is marketed as taming dangerous food and bringing body and mind to healthful fulfillment.

The most effective spokespersons for nutritionism were women concerned with aiding impoverished people in the slums of Northern industrial cities and particularly with reforming what were thought to be their bad habits. In the final decades of the nineteenth century, the Woman's Education Association, formed in Boston, tried to instruct working-class and immigrant families in thrift, temperance, and hygiene. Such associations were part of a larger program that became known as the Settlement Movement, which reflected the rise of social work and concern with the conditions and behavior of the poor. The movement intervened in many constructive ways to improve schools, set up community centers, demand political reform, and improve sanitation. The reformers' nutritional ideas have not stood up well over time, however.

The food program of the Woman's Education Association, established to teach thrifty and nutritional cooking, was called the New England Kitchen. Its members offered what they considered a modern cuisine based on scientific principles and aligned to reform of personal conduct. Poor people could be taught to feed their families cheaply and with improved nutritional results. It was considered ridiculous, for example, that Italian immigrants preferred cooking with olive oil when butter was less expensive and better for you; and why were American-born working families so fond of oysters when mackerel was much cheaper? The New England Kitchen promoted a plain diet that rejected spices, pickles, and other piquant flavorings in favor of white sauces, white bread, oatmeal, potatoes, codfish, sugar, and dairy products. Their recommendations tended to be bland and minimally adorned.

The science of the time was in fact wrong. It turns out that meat and milk are not miracle foods and that vegetables are nutritionally valuable, but as is often the case, persuasive pseudo-facts were more important than actual ones. If the constituents of dietary advice have changed, the overall nexus of self-denial and self-improvement has strengthened and spread from its original center in the United States all over the world. Confusion over what constitutes a healthful diet is caused less by conflicting nutritional advice and more by our reluctance to accept it. There is in fact no conflict over recommendations that we eat less, exercise more, and avoid snacks, processed convenience food, fast food—but these instructions are annoying. The wish to eat what one wants and yet maintain glowing good health has provided two openings for the food industry: to assert that their products are actually healthful when they aren't—Froot Loops with a heart-healthy endorsement—and to substitute chemical ingredients such as artificial sweeteners or "lite" versions of cheese and yogurt and claim they are great-tasting. These reconcile health and desire by means of dubious assertions.

Food-related health concerns are expressed in scientific language, but they arise as much from a spiritual and cultural outlook as from nutritional evidence. In magazines and online sites, advice on avoiding illness and promoting wellness reflects anxiety over everyday life, especially the experience of stress. Fears of foods involving sugar, gluten, and chemical additives have varying degrees of validity, but they all stem from an effort to cope with modern life and its nervous over-stimulation and rushing around that induces people to embrace New Age teachings or to declutter, discover herbal teas, or engage in Yoga. The feeling that you are caring for your body reinforces a fragile, or frazzled, sense of caring for the soul as well as an impression of control.

Another cultural aspect of diet is related to body image. It is widely believed, but untrue, that hierarchically arranged societies in which many people are hungry admired bulk as a sign of privilege. Gluttony and obesity are seldom regarded with approval. Standards of beauty are indeed changeable, however. The heroines of medieval romance were thin, pale, and delicate, while the late-nineteenth-century American female was supposed to have a full figure. *How to Be Plump* is the title of a physician's book published in 1878 addressed to women who did not want to look meager. Around the same time, the University of Chicago proudly announced in its publicity that nearly all of its female students gained weight over the course of an academic year.

Beginning with the Gibson Girl of the 1890s, the American feminine ideal became slimmer, more athletic, and women's bodies were less constrained by layers of clothing. By the flapper era, the 1920s, a svelte silhouette reigned. Exercise and a muscular body have become more important in the ensuing hundred years, and the current thin, athletic ideal female figure usually requires discipline, vigilance, and self-sacrifice.

Today there are some well-respected voices calling for a less frantic and adversarial attitude toward food, a more common-sensical approach that allows for preferences and returns to a notion of balance and equilibrium, defined more psychologically than in terms of specific foods. Michael Pollan's advice quoted earlier, to eat food, mostly plants, and not too much, allows for personal tastes and takes some pressure off of constant measurement. The paradox of contemporary issues of food and health is that in a grossly unequal society, you have to be affluent in order to fuss about food and health. A great amount of preventive medical attention is paid to people whose basic lifestyle offers no imminent health challenges, while the less privileged who lack access to care are subject to a diet so unhealthful that diabetes and chronic malnutrition are more widespread than they were fifty years ago.

6

women, men, and food

Making cake is not a man's job.

—CAROLINE FRENCH BENTON,
*THE FUN OF COOKING: A
STORY FOR BOYS AND GIRLS,*
1915

Before the Industrial Revolution, feeding a less crowded but also less technologically advanced planet required a minimum of eighty percent of the total population to engage in acquiring food, through hunting, agriculture, fishing, or raising livestock. Societies have allocated different roles and spaces to men and women so that, for example, in much of West Africa, market women take on the job of selling food, while in pre-modern Europe women sold only certain commodities—fish but not meat; raw and spun wool but usually not cloth. In the pre-modern European countryside, women were responsible for the home and its surroundings, while men labored in outlying fields or in craft occupations such as milling and blacksmithing. Women's work had indisputable economic value. In medieval England, tending dairy cattle, gardening, keeping hens, and making ale were female responsibilities. Men were occupied with the outer economy of the village: plowing and sowing the fields, ditching, cutting trees, and maintaining fences. The wheat harvest, which had to be accomplished as quickly as possible to avoid allowing rain and rot to spoil the crop, involved every able-bodied person, male and female.

A medieval song contrasts men's and women's tasks, a husband and wife each complaining that the other does not know what real work is. The man's labor is hard and monotonous and takes place unprotected from the weather. The wife's jobs are more varied, too much so, ranging from spinning wool to childcare to churning butter. The couple agree to trade chores for a day to see who is right, but lamentably we do not know who won the argument because the poem's conclusion has been lost.

Every society has arranged family labor differently, so it is not surprising that indigenous customs should have seemed unfamiliar, even unnatural, to European travelers and colonists. English settlers in North America considered it scandalous that Native American women tended crops while the men "merely" hunted and fished. Colonial observers in the seventeenth century regarded the indigenous men's activities as recreational, one noting that "women were generally very laborious at their planting time, and the men extraordinarily idle." It was not that the colonists thought women should not engage in economically productive labor, but it was shocking that crop cultivation should fall to them.

Only much later—for England, during the Victorian era—did wives' domestic work come to be seen as without monetary value, in contrast to male wage or salary labor. Women still took care of the home, but the house, grounds, children, and servants were now regarded as consuming rather than creating productive income. The prevailing notion communicated by the authoritative media was that men were fitted by nature to go out and make their mark on the world while it fell to women, with their tenderhearted character, to make the home a refuge. This latter image was enduringly evoked by Coventry Patmore's poem "The Angel in the House," the first part of which appeared in 1854. The middle-class cult of female domesticity relegated wives to the sweetly supportive role, uninvolved in anything public or monetary other than shopping. Such passivity did not apply to working-class women, who were employed outside the home in textile mills, retail trades, offices, and as servants; moderately affluent women, however, were no longer engaged in anything to do with trade, production, or finance.

The home conceived as comfort for men, the economic actors, meant that preparing meals, along with maintaining the house and seeing to the children, was a wife's responsibility, no longer shared with others as had been the case on farms. In England the man might monitor the wine cellar, and later in the United States the husband handled outdoor cooking, but these pleasurable and occasional tasks had little to do with the daily responsibility of putting food on the proverbial table.

How middle-class women spent their days varied according to whether or not they gave directions to servants, whether they lived in rural or urban settings, and what access to a wider world their individual situation and determination might permit. Nineteenth-century writers devoted a great degree of attention to domesticity and child-rearing. The bourgeois house was a place of culture and art, with a piano, rooms for different functions and times of day, and elaborate décor. Middle-class mothers supervised children more closely than did mothers in wealthy households whose offspring were placed in the care of nursemaids, governesses, and boarding schools, or lower-class parents who put their children out to wage work at an early age.

Cooking interfered with middle-class female obligations and interests, and this created a market for convenience products and appliances along with simplified meals, especially once servants became unaffordable beginning early in the twentieth century. Notwithstanding the popularity of shared activities such as playing music, games, picnicking, and mixed sports like tennis, men and women spent more time apart than on the old-style farm. Married men were out of the house all day and at all seasons and took many of their meals without their wives' company. Women who stayed home as well as those who worked for a wage came to be acknowledged as having different opinions about food from those of men. The gendering of taste may have been a result of more sophisticated consumer desires and a growing ethos of personal fulfillment.

Assumptions about male and female food predilections are so ingrained that they are hardly noticed. Hiding in plain sight are expectations that women are more preoccupied with dieting, more likely to be vegetarian, more worried about health altogether. Men are widely assumed to like meat in general, steak in particular, and such things as hot sauce or milk, while women are supposed to prefer light and insubstantial food, but also desserts, chocolate, and candy.

There are actually few ageless associations of women with particular food habits. That women experience strange cravings during pregnancy does have a long literary as well as medical history. Athenaeus in the *Deipnosophistae* notes that the geographer Polemon says that before giving birth to Apollo, Leto passionately desired a certain type of horn-shaped onion. In Christopher Marlowe's play

Doctor Faustus, written around 1590, the pregnant duchess of Vanholt craves ripe grapes in winter, and Faustus employs his diabolically bestowed powers to procure them. Offered as an example of the puerile use Faustus makes of his bargain with the devil, the duchess's whim needs no explaining.

Female partiality to sweets may not be quite as venerable as the desires during pregnancy, but the notion goes back at least four hundred years. Earlier, when sugar was rare and credited with medicinal properties, it was consumed by the powerful and prestigious in the manner of spices and lacked gendered identification. Princely banquets ended with sugar-coated nuts, fruit, or spices (a category known as *comfits*). Medicinal spices or pharmacological preparations were made with sugar into jellies or lozenges called *electuaries,* sugar being a vehicle for ingesting otherwise unpalatably bitter ingredients. Comfits and electuaries are the ancestors of candy. At a papal election held in Avignon in January 1371, the twenty or so cardinals enjoyed twelve pounds of candied spices before retiring to their conclave. No one yet seems to have thought of women as uniquely enraptured by sweets.

With the growing availability of sugar in Europe, thanks to the exploitation of the Caribbean islands, sweet-tasting items were feminized. The Catalan historian Jeroni Pujades (1568–1635) denounced aristocratic young women who ate cakes and pastries in public locations. Nicolas de Bonnefons and Sir Hugh Platt, authors of seventeenth-century confectionary recipes, dedicated their book to "ladies" and/or "gentlewomen."

Extending beyond aristocratic circles, ice cream was the sweet creation most responsible for feminizing the imagery of sugar.

Beginning in the late eighteenth century, ice cream was an attraction at pleasure gardens, privately run parks with entertainment, food, and drink. The exemplar was London's Vauxhall Gardens, opened in 1785 and thereafter widely imitated, from St. Petersburg in Russia to Philadelphia in the United States. Payment of an entrance fee provided a chance to admire tightrope walkers and to enjoy concerts, hot air balloons, and other diversions. Along with coffee, cakes, and chocolate, ice cream was available as a refined but convivial comestible. Part of the popularity of pleasure gardens was that they provided opportunities for men and women to mingle without prior, parentally sanctioned acquaintance.

In the first years of the nineteenth century, ice cream became a retail and restaurant item, sold in what were referred to as "ice cream houses" or "ice cream saloons." Wendy A. Woloson, an authority on sugar consumption and social habits in this era, points out that already in 1809, a male observer calling himself *Fornax* (furnace in Latin), warned that women's unreasonable fondness for ice cream was dangerous. He claimed that just the other day, a young lady had fainted coming out of an ice cream house after consuming two or three glasses of "this cold, pernicious composition."

By cutting blocks of ice in winter and erecting storage structures to keep it through the summer, it became possible to make ice cream available during the hot months when it was most desired. Until the end of the nineteenth century when electric refrigeration was invented, ice cream was a luxury, but not so expensive as to discourage middle-class customers. It was an affordable, routine indulgence, equivalent to Starbucks lattés or

Shake Shack hamburgers, readily consumed in great quantities by those with extra but not unlimited money to spend.

Ice cream saloons were designed as primarily female spaces. Parkinson's in Philadelphia or Thompson's in New York were decorated with gilt and mirrors and strategically located near shopping locales, particularly department stores. These non-alcoholic saloons provided much more than ice cream, their menus offering game and roast meat, but their business was based on elegant sweets that women were commonly supposed to adore. As with the pleasure gardens, such establishments were objects of moral censure. Since they did not prohibit male patrons, the ice cream saloons were thought to encourage illicit or at least unseemly social intercourse.

After the Civil War, a vogue for carbonated beverages offered by soda fountains replaced the ice cream saloons. Beginning as adjuncts to pharmacies and dispensing putatively medicinal drinks, drugstore soda fountains became popular in the 1870s and 1880s when they added flavors and ice cream to soda water. Sugary drinks, the image of healthfulness, and the tasteful décor attracted women and, once again, sanctioned or unsanctioned courting and sociability followed.

Other than a partiality for sweetness and the special case of pregnancy, however, women were not thought to have different food tastes from men until the late nineteenth century. Neither, for that matter, did children merit special kinds of food or consideration once they were no longer babies. Before the 1860s, cookbooks in Europe and the United States were brimming with tips on how to treat servants, devise home remedies for ailments, or get rid of insects, but in all this prolix discourse nothing implied gendered food preferences. Cookbooks addressed to the housewife assumed that the family would appreciate her efforts.

Surveys around 1900, however, show that already male and female college students had developed different eating habits. Male students ate more meat and in a greater variety of cuts. At Western Reserve University in Cleveland, the matron in charge of the women's residence ordered precut meat, while the male dormitory supervisor bought meat by the side or quarter. Like the male students, the women ate bacon and ham, but only the men seem to have been fond of pork chops, loin, ribs, and sausages. The female students had more varied and adventurous menus: forty-seven kinds of vegetables were prepared at their dining hall as opposed to fourteen for the men.

Around the same time, restaurants started to come up with dishes other than ice cream that were intended to appeal to women's newly identified partiality to light entrées. Today "light" denotes non-filling and low-calorie dishes: salads, fish, vegetables. The word "dainty" covered much of the same ground at the beginning of the twentieth century, with the additional meaning of decorative. Women were supposed to like insubstantial but kaleidoscopic food effects such as a medley of Jell-O colors or a tropical fruit salad topped with shredded coconut. Further ornamental touches could be added using artificial coloring, mayonnaise swirls, canned mandarin oranges, or whipped cream.

As employed in women's magazines and other media, dainty was usually a term of praise. In Syracuse, New York, the first branch of what would become the Schrafft's chain of restaurants described itself in 1906 as "the daintiest luncheon spot in all the state." On the other hand, when confronted with the imperative that wives please their husbands, dainty was used contemptuously. In 1934, *House and Garden* warned its readers, "Keep your dainties for women's luncheons." Marshmallow-date whip may be fine for such occasions, the article went on, but your husband is likely to stray if you try such dishes on him. Men were supposed to be fond of meat, spicy food, fried food, anything with an assertive flavor. Examples provided were chili, curry, mutton chops, and Roquefort cheese. A whole genre of cookbooks between 1910 and 1960 purported to tell women how to keep their husbands happy, books with titles like *A Thousand Ways to Please a Husband,* published in 1917.

It was not only daintiness that men disdained. They presented themselves as defenders of real food as opposed to women's susceptibility to the blandishments of convenience. Women were blamed for the mediocrity of American food because they had been seduced by cans, mixes, packaged goods, and flavorless novelties. At the end of the 1930s, researchers for "America Eats," a never-completed government-funded (WPA) project to report on American foodways, were told to concentrate on community celebrations such as clambakes, pig roasts, barbecues, and fish fries. They should ignore domestic household preparations because women's proclivities for embellished but tasteless, easy-to-make food had so undermined culinary traditions that home cooking was no longer worth exploring.

Enamored of dainty, bright, colorful effects and bland processed food, women were typified by male food writers as basically uninterested in the pleasures of dining because of the drudgery of cooking and their preoccupation with dieting. This is a recurring stereotype in twentieth-century cookbooks written for men, which bragged about male creativity and fondness for authentic and lusty fare, rejecting "sissy," insipid, and over-garnished dishes. Deshler Welch, author of *The Bachelor and the Chafing Dish* (1896), perhaps the first cookbook addressed to men, opined that "Men cook to please themselves and women cook to please others." Left to themselves, he went on, women would be perfectly happy with tea and toast because food bores them.

As late as 1972 Thomas Mario, author of *The Playboy Gourmet,* affected to pity women who are compelled to "a sadly repetitive . . . get-it-done-by-six-o'clock job." Bachelors, on the other hand, are passionate and excited about food because, cooking for pleasure and not necessity, they can follow impulses, improvise, and not be confined to the recipe's directions. Why not try potatoes Lorette, whose contrast of crisp exterior and creamy interior, "like the snatches of a light Parisian song, remind him of a magnificent dinner he once ate on the Boulevard St. Germain?" That Parisian meal probably did not feature quiche, as just five years after *The Playboy Gourmet,* the best-selling *Real Men Don't Eat Quiche* appeared, its snappy sexist title requiring no explanation.

In recent decades, binary male-female identities have been creatively complicated, yet certain ideas about gendered food preferences remain strong. In the heyday of postwar suburbia, when the advertisers' image of the housewife ruled the airwaves, men cooked meat outdoors. This was their particular space because the techniques were presented as closer to male-oriented activities like camping and tinkering with machinery than the indoor, un-dramatic female preoccupation with vacuuming and baking. President Eisenhower shared his recipe for steak grilled right on top of glowing coals, and this association of men and grilling is by no means an American peculiarity. In the 1979 film *Moscow Does Not Believe in Tears,* one of the male characters observes (accord-ing the English subtitles): "Shashlik [grilled kebabs on skewers] does not tolerate women's hands."

American men to this day are thought of as fond of grilling, and they supposedly also like hot sauce and experimental concoc-tions, while women are typified as enamored of vegetables and chocolate desserts. Women are the pacesetters of current food campaigns, however, just as they led the nutritionists of the late nineteenth century and the farm-to-table movement that began in the 1970s. Vegetarianism, veganism, and their equivocal but popular "vegetable-forward" cousin are all ascendant trends as-sociated with women. One could say that of the two wings of the effort to decrease meat consumption, men support the artificial solution (Impossible Burger and the like) and women the vege-tarian side; they would be happy getting rid of both the burger and its imitators.

So far, we have been concerned with cooking at home. Perhaps the oddest aspect of the peculiar history of food and gender, how-ever, is the division between home and restaurant. Although women are largely responsible for domestic meals, cooking in res-taurants is done overwhelmingly by men, both in ordinary estab-lishments as well as at the celebrity end of the spectrum. It would be hard to come up with another occupational category like this, partly because other male-dominated jobs (airline pilot, chemist, investment banker) have no domestic parallel. Doctors, until recently, were overwhelmingly male, while women were usually in charge of the family's routine health matters, but today thirty-six percent of medical doctors are female, and women make up over half the students in medical schools.

Given the tradition of male chefs' domination, it is remarkable that the French culinary repertoire applies feminine adjectival forms to sauces and cooking styles. It is Béarnaise sauce, not Béarnais; the classic fish-stock sauce is matelote (the sailor's wife), not matelot (the sailor); even financière rather than financier for a Madeira and truffle sauce. The famous tuna salad is Niçoise; macaroni might be à l'Italienne, or à la Sicilienne. Specific preparation styles might be named in honor of men (à la Rothschild; Boeuf Wellington), but the default gender is feminine. Perhaps this is part of the upgrading of rustic dishes mentioned earlier in discussing high and low cuisines. The miller's wife is credited with inventing a butter sauce ("meunière") or the addition of curry makes anything "à l'Indienne." The ultimate repository of cooking techniques is female and based on the household, but its retailing and professionalization are masculine.

Apart from this representation of female origination, there have been times and places where professional female chefs achieved notice. The city of Lyons, for example, has a tradition of female restaurant proprietors going back to the mid-eighteenth century. La Mère Guy (Mother Guy) was famous for her eel stew, and in 1759 she opened a modest establishment to commercialize it. Françoise Fillioux (1865–1925), proprietress of Le Bistrot Fillioux, was the first celebrated representative of what in the Belle Époque were being called "Les Mères Lyonnaises." She was ferociously jealous of her star apprentice, Eugénie Brazier, who did indeed surpass all others, becoming in 1938 the first chef, male or female, to acquire three Michelin stars for two restaurants, both called La Mère Brazier, one in Lyons and the other to the west in a village called Col de la Luère. Not until 1998 did Alain Ducasse repeat this accomplishment.

In the United States as well there were always female chefs and restaurateurs. *The Culinarians,* a compendium of 175 short biographies by David Shields, identifies fourteen women who were either chefs, caterers, or restaurateurs active between the 1790s and the implementation of Prohibition in 1920. In my book *Ten Restaurants That Changed America* (2016), four out of the ten were started by women: Mamma Leone's, an Italian restaurant in New York established by Louisa Leone in 1906; the Mandarin in San Francisco, created by Cecilia Chiang in 1961; Sylvia's, a Southern/soul food place in Harlem opened by Sylvia Woods in 1962; and Alice Waters's Chez Panisse in Berkeley (1971). Nevertheless, in 2019 only seven percent of fine dining restaurants in the United States had female chefs, while the overwhelming majority of meals at home were still prepared by women.

In the long and not completely propitious history of female restaurant chefs, *Time* magazine's "The Gods of Food" article in November 2013 represents a point of inflection. The cover featured the top "dudes of food": René Redzepi, Alex Atala, and David Chang. Just below them, thirteen chefs were named to the "Pantheon," all men. Below these were "influencers," again including only male chefs. Even the historical lineage or "family tree" left out figures like Alice Waters and the modernist Catalan chef Carme Ruscalleda. *Time*'s deifications provoked both mirth and anger.

The #MeToo movement has toppled male chef-idols from their plinths and made it impossible to sustain the macho, loud, irrepressible rascal image. As a caution against too much enthusiasm, however, the triumph of the female chef has been heralded before, with disappointing results. "We thought everything was going to change," Ruth Reichl said about the late 1970s and early 1980s when Alice Waters, Judy Rodgers, and Evan Kleiman broke through the barriers to fame. Insofar as female chefs in the 1990s and beyond were grudgingly given some space, it was as nurturers and keepers of homey traditions, while the men were lauded as iconoclastic geniuses.

The bias toward male chefs as artists reflects the persistence of twentieth-century truisms about male risk-taking and creativity in the kitchen, as opposed to women's dutiful, literal, and unreflective meal preparation. Molecular gastronomy, which first attained global fame with Ferran Adrià in the late 1990s, reinforced this contrast. Not that every great figure of modernist cuisine is by any means obnoxious. A few, like Massimo Bottura of Osteria Francescana in Modena, are actually likeable. After all, he wrote a cookbook with the self-deprecating title *Never Trust a Skinny Italian Chef.* Others, like René Redzepi, are doing something about the prejudicial ecological and social effects of food. What the 2013 food gods and their successors share is inspiration and a revolutionary spark that until recently was widely presented as an exclusively male attribute.

Turning from women as chefs to women as customers, they have been patrons since the modern form of the restaurant first took shape in Paris 250 years ago, but female participation was restricted or regulated to certain times of day or to particular settings. Long before restaurants existed, private dinners too were subject to rules about female attendance. Plato's *Symposium* and the sophists' endless dinner in Athenaeus were all-male events, except for what Athenaeus constantly refers to as "flute girls" and other female entertainers. Roman feasts were for the diversion of men, but likely to include women as part of the performance.

The unremarked and lubricious role of women at celebratory dining occasions anticipates the presence of what were deemed disreputable women at officially all-male parties. In the nineteenth and early twentieth centuries, restaurant owners justified segregating or banning upstanding women by claiming to protect them from being accosted as if they were prostitutes.

In nineteenth-century Europe and North America, women deemed respectable were welcomed at least sometimes and in some places, especially at night and in the company of men. Nowhere before the 1860s were women commonly allowed to dine alone or in all-female groups, except to the degree that hotels and other public establishments set aside what was called in the United States a "Ladies' Ordinary," where women traveling or for some other reason obligated to dine alone could be accommodated in a way that avoided men's leering and harassment.

Countries and cultures differed as to what restaurant space women might be offered, ideally something affording a degree of privacy but without being shut off from public view. In Paris there were few restrictions. British and American visitors in the early part of the nineteenth century were astonished by opulent dining locales where women ate, drank, laughed, and admired themselves in vast mirrors. In the 1830s and 1840s, certain Parisian restaurants provided private dining rooms with inconspicuous entrances.

New York imitated Paris, although with more cynicism. The city's "private supper rooms," beginning in the 1840s, were unpublicized but ubiquitous. Attached to regular restaurants, they had their own doorways and only male-female couples were allowed; a single man or group of men could not reserve one of these rooms merely for the sake of ordinary privacy. The food and drink charges might be as much as double the prices stated on the restaurant's normal bill of fare. The facilities consisted of a small dining room where anything could be ordered at any time of night, and an adjoining bedroom.

San Francisco restaurants too profited from the association of sex with dining. With the Gold Rush, lonely men with money to spend poured into the city, and restaurants arranged monetized opportunities for female companionship. Elegant San Francisco establishments such as the Poodle Dog constructed intimate dining rooms. Impromptu, no-reservations socializing in the main dining area was also possible. In the 1860s notorious women like Boston Sal or The Girl in Green mingled with male customers at the finest restaurants. In a reversal of the common pattern, San Francisco restaurateurs recommended private rooms to married couples in order to avoid the raucous omnium-gatherum of the public areas.

In London, the high-end restaurant was not introduced until the 1860s, but here too what were called *cabinets particuliers* were set aside (French being useful for both gastronomy and seduction). In H. G. Wells's *Ann Veronica,* published in 1909, the heroine shares a meal with a married man at one of these bijou dining retreats. After the waiter has set out the food, poured the wine, and departed, Ann's escort locks the door and attempts to rape her. When she fights him off, he reproaches her for affecting innocence when she has accompanied him to the opera and a private dinner arranged for an obvious purpose.

Escorted by husbands or other respectable male companions, women were graciously accommodated in the evening at British and American restaurants. Newspaper and magazine accounts rhapsodized over the jewels, dresses, and beauty of the ladies dining with men at places like Delmonico's in New York or the Saint Charles Hotel in New Orleans. Lunch at high-end restaurants, however, was for men only, and many London venues as late as 1895 displayed placards stating that ladies would not be served between noon and three o'clock in the afternoon.

By the end of the Civil War, American restaurants were willing to set aside rooms for women who wanted to dine together. Succeeding decades saw a proliferation of restaurants designed to provide lunch for female office and retail workers alone or in small groups. Unlike the earlier ice cream saloons, these were not elegant and expensive but clean, simple, and safe—lunchrooms like Childs, which started in 1889 and expanded rapidly in the early twentieth century. By the 1930s there were more than forty Childs restaurants in New York and at least a hundred in the United States and Canada. Their glazed tile walls and white tables looked hygienic, an impression reinforced by the nurse-like uniforms of the waitresses.

By 1900 women and men could mingle at all times of day without giving rise to comment. In Britain, Colonel Nathaniel Newnham-Davis wrote a series of restaurant reviews for the *Pall Mall Gazette* that were collected in *Dinners and Diners: Where and How to Dine in London* (1899). Newnham-Davis delighted in female companionship when he visited celebrated establishments such as the Hotel Savoy, as well as modest Soho French and Italian spots and even a kosher restaurant. The colonel found it quite unremarkable that groups of women should dine at these places without any male escort.

In both the City of London and the West End, one given over to work, the other oriented around leisure and entertainment, the beginning of the twentieth century saw a sharp increase in the number and variety of inexpensive and informal restaurants. Women and men now had lunch near offices or shops. Particularly popular were vegetarian spots and chain restaurants such as ABC (the initials stood for "Aerated Bread Company") and Lyons. Beginning as a tea shop, Lyons had 150 branches in London by 1910. Its success was the result of its ability to provide reliable gentility at an attractive price for a wide spectrum of customers. The common sight of men and women having lunch together or women in groups or alone signaled a crucial change at the beginning of the twentieth century.

The United States evolved in a fashion similar to the United Kingdom. High-end restaurants were run for the convenience of men, admitting women on sufferance. The free lunch bar (where food was subsidized by beer and liquor consumption), the working man's café, and the diner were also male preserves. Women had teahouses, ice cream saloons, and utilitarian or genteel lunch establishments. A new category of middle-class restaurants served men and women without overt discrimination. The United States had a wide range of middle-class options, including sandwich shops, luncheonettes, drugstore soda fountains, roadside establishments, and places serving foreign cuisine. Such restaurants provided a less rule-bound and hierarchical dining experience than what formal restaurants dictated. Chinese restaurants were notably unconcerned with either upper- or lower-class social rules and were among the first to allow African American and white patrons to intermingle.

Mid-level eating places received indirect encouragement from the Volstead Act, the constitutional amendment enacted in 1919 and repealed in 1933 that banned alcoholic drinks. In destroying the fine-dining restaurant that had depended on sales of wine and liquor, Prohibition created opportunities for less pretentious categories where the often mediocre food was at least inexpensive, convenient, and not tied to alcohol.

In the twentieth century, the number of restaurant types increased as did the absolute number of places to dine out. No longer the preserve of a social elite or of urban Bohemians, restaurants became favored gathering spaces. As will be discussed in connection with forms of conviviality, restaurants would come to define much of our celebratory as well as discriminatory (in both senses of the word) attitudes.

7

race

What's the difference between soul
and southern food? I get asked that
question a lot.

—ADRIAN MILLER, *SOUL
FOOD*

E thnicity, income, and gender affect what people eat. The notion that vegetarianism is feminine, for example, or that only Swedes and Norwegians like *lutefisk* (gelatinous fermented fish) amount to more than odd epiphenomena. They are part of the personal and collective orientation around food described earlier. This chapter looks at race, another way of structuring the everyday significance of food in history. What follows considers African Americans as the authors and agents of food culture.

The enslavement of Africans and their transport to the Americas had varying culinary effects. Discussing the food of the British North American colonies, the food historian James E. McWilliams identified regions whose distinct cuisines were determined less than one would expect by climate or environment and more by the extent of slavery and the type of agricultural economy. The Caribbean islands, the mainland South, the mid-Atlantic, and New England differed as to the proportion of the enslaved population and, as a result, the nature of their culinary evolutions.

In the seventeenth and the first half of the eighteenth century, British entrepreneurs and the government made far more money from the West Indies than from any other part of the expanding empire. By the late seventeenth century, islands like Barbados and Antigua were given over to sugar cultivation and more than seventy-five percent of their inhabitants were enslaved people from Africa. The sugar plantation owners were not interested in making a permanent home in what they considered an unhealthful climate, any more than American oil technicians today expect to put down roots in Angola or Saudi Arabia. Planters intended to make as much money as possible as quickly as they could and return home in triumph to their native territory.

Although relentless in their pursuit of profit, planters could not simply starve the men and women they enslaved. The workers had to be fed, and it proved more economical and less troublesome to give the slaves land to raise their own food than to spend money to provide them with expensive biscuits, dried fish, and salt meat from Europe. As long as the slaves were going to be allowed to fish, catch animals, and cultivate edible plants, their masters figured they might as well eat what the slaves were cooking. Not only were imported hardtack and salt pork costly, they often arrived in poor condition after a long voyage.

Not surprisingly then, the cuisine of the Caribbean is the closest to Africa of any in North America. The slave trade brought over products of African origin such as okra, sorghum, watermelon, and yams, as well as staples originally from Asia such as bananas, plantains, and rice that were already circulating in Africa. Enslaved cooks used American starches such as corn and cassava and adapted Native American methods for cooking turtles and fish. Some New World items like cassava eventually became more important in Africa through commerce with the New World than they had been in the Americas.

European accounts of West Indian food describe a multitude of ingredients mixed into stews and soups. Lady Maria Nugent, the wife of the lieutenant governor of Jamaica, kept a journal of her stay on the island during the first years of the nineteenth century. She refers to hog cooked in the manner of the "maroons" (runaway slaves), crab pepper pot with okra, turtle soup, crab cakes, and another soup made from parrots, okra, and lots of spices (she particularly emphasizes allspice). She was impressed although displeased: "It was all astonishing as it was disgusting."

West African methods of cooking favored slow simmering of soupy rather than thick stews, flavored with spices such as malagueta pepper and later one of the most globally successful American ingredients, chili peppers. Meat and fish were roasted separately or added to stews in pieces. The basic starches were cassava, sorghum, and green plantains, often boiled and pounded into dough-like consistency.

Caribbean versions of African as well as Native American cooking practices involved one-container dishes such as pepper pot, fish head stew, and callaloo, the latter consisting of wild greens, okra, and seafood. Slaves invented other combinations of European and African ingredients. Ackee, now the national dish of Jamaica, centers around a red, globe-shaped fruit brought over from Africa, sautéed with salt cod, and most often served at breakfast. In the colonial era, the salt cod would have come from New England.

In contrast to the Caribbean entrepreneurs, the early English settlers of New England were fleeing religious repression and had completely different expectations of the New World, wishing to become self-sufficient farmers rather than to develop a profitable export crop. Although the New England colonies did have enslaved African laborers (roughly 10 percent of Rhode Island's population in 1750, for example), the economy was not entirely dependent on them and their influence on the development of local cuisine was much less than was the case for the tropical islands.

The relatively small population of African origin does not mean the colonists in Massachusetts or Connecticut simply transplanted the cooking they had grown up with, however. Much as they would have liked to replicate the English diet based on wheat, beef, ale, and dairy products, the settlers who arrived in seventeenth-century New England faced a climate different from that of England and had to create their own livestock industry. Wheat did not thrive and although plenty of game was available, domestic animal meat and milk remained scarce. The colonists were forced to take up Native American practices and products in order to survive. Farmers and those they fed depended on New World food like pumpkins, wild turkeys, and above all maize, which was referred to as *Indian corn* (the English meaning of *corn* being wheat). What in accord with current American usage we will refer to as "corn" was a versatile staple that could be made into pancakes, porridge, or a crumbly sort of bread.

New England was teeming with natural bounty, but much of it failed to impress the settlers. Corn flourished. But even though it is quite nutritious, it was despised as were clams, cranberries, and other native products. The diversified Indian systems of shifting agriculture, hunting, fishing, and foraging were regarded as inferior to the settled, organized, non-improvised regime of row crops, domesticated animals, and letting specialists take care of fishing and hunting. The Protestant settlers' ideal "city on a hill" was planned to be surrounded by fields and meadows, and its inhabitants were supposed to eat pork chops and wheat bread.

The lack of an export crop meant that the settlers could devote themselves to creating a sustainable supply of locally grown food, and eventually to profit from the wealth of the West Indies by replacing the English as distillers of rum from molasses and as suppliers of food such as salted beef, salted cod, and manufactured products. New England was closer and easier to reach from those islands than Britain, and the northern colonies entered into a period of conflict with the mother country over this lucrative trade, one of the causes of the American Revolution. Sugar refining and rum manufacture were particularly important in New England and the mid-Atlantic. New England rum was shipped not only to the West Indies, but also to Africa where it was used as payment for slaves transported to the sugar islands of the Caribbean.

By the mid-eighteenth century, affluence allowed New Englanders to edge away from dependence on corn and other Native American foods. They now had enough incoming revenue to afford to buy wheat from mid-Atlantic states like Pennsylvania where its cultivation flourished. Well-off colonists renounced crude, dark maple syrup or molasses in favor of refined white sugar and spices, wine, tea, and other luxuries imported from

England. The comfortable classes of Massachusetts and Connecticut were unlike the Caribbean planters not only in their diversified and self-sustaining agriculture, but in their ability to mimic the English diet rather than depending on slave adaptations of African, Native, and European cuisines. New England was enmeshed in the business of slavery—companies headquartered in Rhode Island controlled much of the eighteenth-century slave trade—but its cuisine was only minimally influenced by Africa.

Between the two extremes of the Caribbean and New England, the mid-Atlantic, Carolinas, and Southern coastal regions were intermediate points in terms of how much the cuisine was affected by slavery. The slave economy was common from Delaware to Florida, but there was a more diverse agricultural system than in the West Indies. There were many independent and subsistence farmers, and the wealthy plantation owners who grew rice, indigo, tobacco, and later, in the post-independence period, cotton, planned to stay permanently on their estates, unlike the West Indian sugar magnates.

As in the Caribbean, enslaved workers of the American South were encouraged to feed themselves, and some were selected to cook for their owners. African influence affected how basic dishes like those made with rice or beans took shape. South Carolina hoppin' John and perlow (a chicken, sausage, and rice preparation) and Louisiana jambalaya are examples. North Carolina was the center of barbecue, particularly slow roasted, highly spiced pork, put together from various culinary cultures by enslaved Africans but eaten by everyone. Sarah Frances Hicks Williams, the wife of a North Carolina state legislator, wrote to her parents in the North not long before the Civil War about "the famous 'barbecue' of the South & which I believe they esteem above all dishes," defining it as roasted pig dressed with red pepper and vinegar.

Not all of the South was equally affected by slavery. Independent white farmers occupied hilly or mountainous country unsuited for large-scale agriculture, making use of few or no slaves. In the states of what would become the Confederacy there were areas in which the vast majority of the population was black and others, like the Appalachian mountain country, where there were few inhabitants of African descent. In the 1900 census, ninety-four percent of the inhabitants of Issaquena County, in the cotton-growing Mississippi Delta, were black. The same census found no black inhabitants in ten southern Appalachian counties.

The fertile, flat, alluvial land of slavery and commercial crops developed a complex cuisine, with African and Native American elements joined to the plantation owners' desire to replicate upper-class English food. The culinary building blocks were corn, rice, pork, fish, and game. Wealthy elements of the white population imitated English clothing fashions, furniture, and silver, as well as luxury cuisine, especially alcoholic punches and syllabubs, and sugary and sweet-spiced desserts. They created an opulent way of life rather than, as it were, merely camping out and awaiting enough profit to move back to England.

The culinary center of the late colonial and early national eras was the mid-Atlantic, from Philadelphia to northern Virginia. This territory witnessed a combination of influences—Native American, West Indian, African, English, German, and French. A high-end cuisine that developed in ports like Baltimore and

Philadelphia was taken up by the elites of New York, Boston, Charleston, and other cities to the north and south. The most luxurious and prestigious dishes of the nineteenth century were terrapins (a species of midsize turtle) cooked as a stew or soup, and canvasback ducks roasted and served with celery sauce and hominy. The best specimens of both came from the Chesapeake Bay, and many other products from its shores and estuaries, ranging from lamb and mutton to oysters and crabs, were renowned and shipped to distant locales. Late-nineteenth-century banquets in Montana began with East Coast oysters; the Pacific Union Club in San Francisco offered terrapin à la Maryland.

In the early nineteenth century, African American chefs and caterers were exponents and promoters of mid-Atlantic gourmet cuisine. Philadelphia terrapin cookery got its start with a series of African American "public waiters," as they were called—in effect accomplished servants for hire who became full-fledged caterers and restaurant owners. Many among the city's black population came from the Caribbean and brought with them a British West Indian cooking style. They also established networks with African American coastal fishermen and trappers who supplied live terrapins and other shoreline bounty. Up to the end of the eighteenth century, Caribbean green turtles were the gourmands' choice, and the arrival at the port of New York or Philadelphia (and London as well) of huge specimens weighing hundreds of pounds was an occasion for feasting. As the giant turtles became scarce, attention turned to the North American terrapin, which, although difficult to dress and cook, was common, succulent, and of manageable size.

The most celebrated Philadelphia terrapin chef and caterer was James Prosser (1782–1861), an African American from New Jersey who opened for business in 1810. He began as a purveyor of green turtle soup, competing against a cartel that divided up selling this luxury item by the days of the week. Fanatical dedication to mastering every aspect of terrapin lore and the delicate points of cookery made Prosser the universally recognized expert. He pioneered the shift from Caribbean green turtles to the mid-Atlantic terrapin, and from soup to a thicker stew or chowder.

In the 1850s a white writer, imitating what he took to be colorful black locution, reported Prosser's detailed advice about terrapins: that they can only be enjoyed when the day is "nippin," for example, meaning that the colder the water the terrapin swims in, the better, the Chesapeake Bay or the Delaware River being superior to the Florida coast. There follow intimidating directions for taking apart and cooking the animal by combining the meat with sherry, egg yolks, and butter. Once it is heated, "Let it simmer gently. Bilin up two or three times does the business. What you are after is to let it blend. There ain't nothing that must be too pointed in terrapin stew. It wants to be a quiet thing, a suave thing . . ."

In the decades before the Civil War, Prosser and other black chefs catered important Philadelphia social events. Prosser owned two restaurants, regarded as among the best in the city. His passing in 1861 was marked by Joseph William Miller's poem "Prosser's Journey to Heaven; or The Triumph of Terrapin," replete with pseudo-dialect and narrating Prosser's adventures in the afterlife. Arriving at the banks of the Styx, Prosser convinces Charon to ferry him across by offering stewed oysters, Jersey sausage, and buckwheat cakes. On the far side of the river, the Furies stop him and refuse the oysters, but are then tamed into docility by means of soft-shell crabs fried in butter and plump reed birds. At the gates of heaven Saint Peter gives Prosser the hardest test. Even canvasbacks and lobster salad fail to move him. It looks hopeless until Prosser mentions terrapin:

> "From salt Del'war's reedy margints,
>   From de shores ob Sheapeake
> Comes our Terrapin, good Petah,
>   Spose o' dem I needn't speak?"

> "What! STEWED TERRAPIN, Jeems Prosser!"
>   Open wide the gates are borne—
> "Here comes Terrapin and Prosser!
>   Make him Welcome as the morn!"

Free black chefs and caterers made successful careers in other cities besides Philadelphia. From 1796 to 1806, Othello Pollard in Boston regularly provided elegant dishes for Harvard College class events. He too was the subject of verses in praise of his food, in this instance cakes rather than terrapin.

For forty years Thomas Downing (1791–1866), an African American originally from the eastern shore of Virginia, was the leading oyster purveyor in New York City, a major distinction in a place that harvested and consumed tons of oysters from its own harbors. With mournful incredulity one reads that East River, Harlem River, and Arthur Kill (Staten Island) oysters were greatly prized. Oysters were unusual in that all classes ate them constantly. They were the most popular street food, often sold at waterfront stands, and at the same time were the expected first course for elegant meals. Downing was particularly famous for supplying pickled oysters.

In 1860, Downing's advocacy before state courts achieved legal recognition of black people as human beings and citizens, in contradiction of the Supreme Court's Dred Scott decision, which had determined them to be property, chattels. His restaurant on Broadway assisted slaves escaping from the South. Both his sons Peter and George were caterers, and George ran the restaurant in the U.S. Congress from 1868 to 1876. He was also active in Newport, Rhode Island, the great summer resort of the Gilded Age.

Enslaved chefs too were accomplished in putting together high-end meals. James Hemings, owned by Thomas Jefferson, learned French culinary skills during Jefferson's time as ambassador in Paris, from 1784 to 1789. The brother of Jefferson's unfree paramour Sally Hemings, James was released from slavery in 1796. James Hemings introduced to America ingredients, techniques, and dishes that he perfected from both French and English inspiration, such as vanilla flavoring, waffles, and bread stuffing.

At Newport, Rhode Island, just before the Civil War, Ward McAllister, a Savannah-born New York socialite, set up a contest between a French chef and a Southern black cook. A "Saratoga Lake" dinner for sixty people included Spanish mackerel, Saratoga potatoes (hot potato chips), soft-shell crabs, woodcock, chicken partridges, and lettuce salad. McAllister declared the Frenchman the winner. He praised the dishes cooked by the enslaved expert but pronounced them lacking in artistry. McAllister and others acknowledged talented African American cooks with a patronizing language that combined admiration for skilled craftsmanship with a certain indulgent contempt.

In the late nineteenth and early twentieth centuries, at the height of the post-Emancipation subjugation of African Americans, it was widely, if sometimes grudgingly, admitted that they had helped build every regional cuisine south of New York. A *New York Times* article on November 10, 1895, went further, stating that, "In so far as we have a National cooking it is of African, rather than European origin." Around the same time, the writer Gaillard Hunt observed: "The professional cooks of the country are Negroes and the national cookery comes from them."

Because of its history of slavery, the region with the most distinctive cuisine in the United States was the South, where after the Civil War, as before, African Americans cooked for themselves and for affluent white families as well. The late nineteenth century witnessed the imposition of harsh subordination through what became known as Jim Crow laws. A parallel marginalization of Southern black culinary tastes advanced, segregating them from white foodways. This separation was largely fictitious: in 1943, a study of black and white Southern households undertaken in connection with enforcement of wartime food rationing found that any difference between what rural whites and African Americans ate was simply because the latter tended to be poorer. "Poor whites eat more like Negroes," the researchers concluded. Nevertheless, the impulse to distinguish food preferences according to race was powerful enough that it was African Americans who came to be associated with collard greens, the nether parts of pigs, chitterlings, and the like.

African American opinion was divided. On one hand, real and imagined distinctive tastes were celebrated as reflecting identity and spirit, like gospel music or the blues. On the other hand, at various times and places black leaders resisted exalting the food of poverty as if it were a sentimental form of solidarity. According to this view, hoe cakes, molasses, fatback, and greens represented indigence, not cultural expression. In the 1890s, Booker T. Washington insisted that students at his Tuskegee Institute in Alabama learn to appreciate a healthful regimen of beef, white bread, Graham crackers, and codfish, based on the advice of emissaries sent by the New England Kitchen, the culinary outreach program of the Woman's Education Association. Washington was practical enough to suggest that local black-eyed peas were an acceptable substitute for Boston baked beans. Fond of Southern delicacies, he was even known to send dressed opossum as a gift, but as part of his gospel of uplift, Washington's institutional dietary policies adhered to the tenets of Northern food reformers.

Progressive African American leaders such as W. E. B. Du Bois rejected Washington's program to mollify white contempt, but they shared his nutritionist opinions. Du Bois was among the first to describe black food culture in serious, sociological terms, but he was wary of presenting an impoverished diet as if it should be cherished. Writing in 1920 in *The Brownies' Book,* a magazine he founded for children, Du Bois repeatedly stated that "there is no such thing as a Negro diet," and "there is no national dish for the colored people." Du Bois agreed with Booker T. Washington that the pitiful regime of salt pork and cornbread had to be improved in light of nutritional science.

The Great Migration of African Americans from the rural South to the urban North, beginning in the 1910s and lasting until the 1960s, brought millions of people into a new setting that both challenged and solidified the association of Southern and African American cooking. Farm traditions such as salting away barrels of pork or barbecuing whole animals could not be replicated in Northern apartment kitchens, and neither were black people already living in New York, Detroit, or Chicago eager to embrace what they saw as "country" food. Migrants' nostalgia for the South's culinary heritage collided with the desire to eat mainstream food that symbolized affluence and modernity.

The migrants' Southern yearning proved to be a marketable alternative to generic luncheonette offerings. Restaurants in Harlem and other Northern centers advertised "Southern" or "Down Home" food, things like grits, fried chicken, barbecued spareribs, turnip greens, and sweet potato pie that catered to the new majority of the population with Southern roots. On the other hand, members of the black elite and those without much in the way of active Southern connections often rejected "down home" as poor, rural, and stereotypic. In *Date with a Dish: A Cook Book of American Negro Recipes* (1948), Freda DeKnight, food columnist for the upscale magazine *Ebony*, ridiculed the widely diffused belief that Southern fried chicken or cornpone epitomized African American cooking. Black people cooked with flair and curiosity, she asserted, going much further than the limits of Southern rural traditions, and in fact, anything cooked by a black person should be considered a "Negro dish." DeKnight did not by any means reject the past, praising ham hocks and including sixteen cornbread recipes, but she asserted that heritage should not be embraced to the detriment of experimentation. *Date with a Dish* presents three tamale pie recipes and instructions for making East Indian chicken as well as Hungarian goulash.

How Southern food is related to African American cuisine remains controversial and is tied up with issues of identity and appropriation. In a chapter of his book *The Cooking Gene* from 2017 entitled "Hating My Soul," Michael W. Twitty lists the foods that black people are supposed to go crazy over, according to a racist song that his father used to play on their hi-fi when he was growing up. The song went on about watermelon, hominy grits, pig tails, chitterlings, collard greens . . . Everyone in the family except his grandfather considered this comical. Twitty remarks that at the time, "I didn't really understand why people ate that shit. Literally, I didn't get it—nobody explained to me the cuisine of want until much later."

What had been an impoverished regional diet became increasingly associated with black people after the Second World War for two reasons: as they became more prosperous, Southern whites changed what they ate; at the same time well-off whites claimed ownership of a category called "Southern Cuisine" with minimal African American influence, so that dishes such as gumbo, grits, or perlow were whitened. Third, black people themselves tended to embrace soul food as a source of distinction.

For some, soul was simply a community-focused way of describing the culinary ground already covered by expressions like "down home" or "Southern." For others, it was an assertion of black nationalism against the integrationist agenda of the civil rights movement in the early 1960s. Sometimes cooking soul food had to be learned because a large percentage of African Americans had not grown up with rural food. Schools in Berkeley, California, taught students how to prepare previously unfamiliar chitterlings, cornbread, and sweet potato pie, often to their parents' confusion and surprise. In the late 1960s and during the 1970s, what had previously been regarded as culinary symbols of oppression were reclaimed for the purposes of cultural pride.

Soul food exalted a certain set of African American dishes but ended their association with the South. No longer were these understood merely as what was eaten in a particular place; they were now embraced in accord with racial and cultural affinity. There were plenty of critiques within the black community, some based on health, others stemming from opposition to praising a cuisine of subordination. Michael W. Twitty reasserts the Southernness of African American food, but through its African origins. This is not a literal culinary return to Africa, but rather an embrace of hybridity and mixture, appropriately expressed by someone who converted to Judaism and sought out his white ancestors and their white descendants.

Twitty describes a series of journeys that evoke memory and connect a real Southern cuisine, black and white, to Africa. He presents the food described in his book as Southern and not exclusively African American, because despite the barriers erected by slavery and segregation, the South has a long history of entangled families and cultures. Rather than there being two types of Southern cooking, one white and one "soul," there is a traumatic but from a culinary point of view rich heritage. Much of the gastronomic history of the past 120 or so years has seen first the whitening of the image of American cuisine and then the slow revelation of the self-serving falsity of this conceit.

False conceits abounded in the evolution of what was regarded as white cuisine. While African Americans were being subjugated by legislation in the post–Civil War South, the traditional foods of New England were rediscovered and transformed as the true, original American cuisine. The First People were allotted a limited, ceremonial role centered around Thanksgiving, but New England cuisine beginning in the 1880s was exalted as the culinary expression of Anglo-Saxon racial superiority.

The English settlers had done their best to end dependence on New World products such as corn, pumpkins, clams, and cranberries, but with the colonial revival of the late nineteenth century these foods were rediscovered. There was new interest in colonial architecture, furniture, and décor and renewed respect for carpenters, cabinet makers, and silversmiths of the eighteenth century. New England started to market itself as a tourist destination, not just for its coastal summer resorts, but for its quaint inns, fall colors, and evocation of early American history. "Indian" pudding (made from cornmeal) and New England boiled dinner became national foods and forgotten regional items like red flannel hash and succotash were marketed across the country. Another manifestation of the gentrification process was the late-nineteenth-century revival of Boston baked beans and pumpkin pie, but the restored versions were sweeter and more elaborate than what went under the same names in colonial times.

In addition to the appeal to nostalgia, New England presented itself as modern, the pioneer of a cooking philosophy that put science before sensual pleasure. As seen in the earlier discussion of health, the virtues of thrift, self-mastery, and nutrition were joined together when it came to teaching working-class and immigrant women how to cook and eat correctly. Nutritionists claimed they were defending goodness, honesty, and the white race. The reception and perversion of Darwin's evolutionary teachings posited a struggle for survival among competing races. According to racialized social theory, the superiority of Caucasians was being undermined by their declining birth rate and tendency to moral decadence as manifested by delayed marriage, gourmandise, homosexuality, and intemperance. The so-called lower races were outpacing white reproduction levels. The most publicized danger was what was called the "Yellow Peril" posed by the teeming masses of China. This kitschy but venomous libel mesmerized both intellectuals and the popular media. The Chinese Exclusion Acts of the 1880s were deemed necessary because the Chinese, an inferior but relentlessly determined race, could work while subsisting on rice and little else, while native-born working man needed meat.

Reforming and perfecting white superiority required moral vigilance but also eugenics, the scientific selection of the best physical and intellectual specimens and limitation of the reproductive capacity of those regarded as deviant or subnormal. According to Ellen Swallow Richards, a nutritionist who was the first woman to graduate from MIT, in order to deal with the dangerous infertility of "the higher branches of the human race," attention had to be paid to what people ate. The diet of American whites was self-indulgent—"pampered" was the term Richards used. She called for a new science of "euthenics" which would advance racial improvement by reforming cooking and housekeeping. New England was the model national cuisine because of its foundational role for the independent United States but also for its frugal food which conformed to an ideology of American enterprise that acclaimed ambition over pleasure and self-control over dissipation.

In contrast to New England, the South became popular as the home of a sensual regional but not national cuisine. Recognition of its culinary distinction was a function of the post–Civil War reorientation by a white Southern leadership determined to return the black population to de facto servitude. In addition to legislation in the 1890s depriving African Americans of the vote, and of equal access to education and to stores, restaurants, and the like, Southern politicians and writers created a cult of the Lost Cause of the Confederacy and manufactured nostalgia for the old plantation and its hospitably chivalrous way of life. It is in this period that Southern food was invented.

Earlier works such as Mary Randolph's *Virginia Housewife* (1824) were not as regionally oriented as their titles make them seem. These were based on (or outright copied) English exemplars, enlivened with a few Southern specialties like okra, sweet potato, or barbecued pig. Randolph was also cosmopolitan, providing recipes for curries, Italian polenta, and Hispanic American shredded pork (*ropa vieja*), as well as food from other parts of the country, for example doughnuts, referred to as "Yankee cakes."

After the Civil War, the South diverged further culturally and economically from the rest of the country. Poor and agrarian rather than industrial, it was stereotyped as backwards. Erskine Caldwell's extremely popular novel *Tobacco Road* from 1932 features child brides, ignorance, cruelty, and deformity. Alternatively, or complementary to this Gothic image, the Old South was suffused with graciousness, epitomized by Margaret Mitchell's *Gone with the Wind.* In keeping with this dichotomy, Southern culinary practices could be represented as, on one hand, a regime of poverty whose overreliance on cornbread produced nutritional disorders like pellagra and rickets or, at the high end, images of splendid hunt balls, mint juleps on the porch, and elaborate dishes brought out on silver trays or chafing dishes by smiling black servants.

The ownership of Southern food has been debated since its invention in the 1870s. Until the 1930s, white opinion tended to acknowledge, even celebrate, the skill of the black kitchen help. For the Caribbean, as Lady Nugent's account of her stay in Jamaica indicates, there was no doubt about who had invented the local cuisine. Some of this accreditation of black culinary skill also characterized the American South. African Americans were presented as uniquely talented.

By the mid-twentieth century, the role of African Americans in Southern cuisine was being eclipsed. Once the fiction of the happy plantation slaves became untenable, it became embarrassing to call attention to subordination. Well into the 1990s, tours of historic plantations made no reference to their African-born former inhabitants, as if the mansion and its gracious way of life ran by itself. Similarly, in food writing, images of happy black subordinates preparing food yielded to elegant dishes appearing out of nowhere.

New Orleans's classic *Picayune Creole Cook Book,* first published in 1900, exemplifies the shift from patronizing celebration of the African American role to setting it aside. Early editions of this publishing success stated that its purpose was to preserve Creole recipes in danger of being lost because former slaves, described as "the old Creole mammies," were passing from the scene. In 1936, however, the eighth edition skipped over the black presence and credited the origins of Creole cuisine to the restaurants of New Orleans. The ninth edition in 1947 replaced the previous cover image, a black woman wearing a headscarf, with the head of a stereotypic French (male) chef with an upturned mustache. Gastronomic and tourist literature during the mid-twentieth century celebrated the Creole cuisine of New Orleans as the product of many influences, French, Spanish, American Indian, German, and Italian, but little or nothing was said about African Americans.

With the recent revival of Southern regional food, Africa is back, although not necessarily for the benefit of African American chefs and restaurateurs. When the white chef Sean Brock visited Senegal, the event was celebrated as if the creator of the Charleston restaurant Husk was, in Michael W. Twitty's simile, a latter-day Dr. Livingstone bringing news from the Dark Continent. An article in Mediaite.com proclaimed "Sean Brock Finds the Origins of Southern Cuisine in Africa." While praising Brock's intentions, Twitty points out that since the mid-twentieth century, black people have been incorporating African cuisine into their understanding of America's food heritage but without receiving reverent media attention.

The way in which African culinary influence becomes visible only if a white authority translates it is complemented by the surprise that greets people of color who do something associated with white activities, like raising organic produce. In 2015 at the fourth MAD Food Symposium in Copenhagen, the Los Angeles urban gardener Ron Finley observed his success with a certain bemusement: "Black man plants a carrot, and the world comes running."

Notwithstanding these persistent racial stereotypes, it is no longer easy to disguise the polyglot origins of what we like and eat. For a time, white people's food was described by the single word *bland,* and terms like *white bread* were used as adjectives for the metaphorically colorless. This is not quite right, however, because certainly since the 1970s, whites have taken to spicy food as well as "ethnic" cuisine. Living in Nashville, Tennessee, from 1979 until 1997, I saw all sorts of highly spiced dishes introduced and popularized, from Buffalo chicken wings to blackened redfish. Later a quirky local specialty, Nashville hot chicken, became an international cult favorite. At Howlin' Ray's, a Nashville hot chicken joint in Los Angeles, there was usually (pre-Covid) a two-hour wait. The Australian chain Belles Hot Chicken invokes Nashville as its inspiration. The story of this invented delicacy is worth outlining as an example of a sequence of accident, transformation, and appropriation.

Hot chicken does not require ingredients available only in Tennessee, nor is it prepared according to some unique folk practice, but it does have a good origins legend. In 1945 an African American named Thornton Prince opened the Barbecue Chicken Shack in the northern part of Nashville. He was, as they used to say, fond of the ladies. According to folklore, his recipe came from his girlfriend who had gotten back at him for coming home one night well after midnight by fixing him some fried chicken, inconspicuously but grossly over-spiced with hot peppers. Her intention to inflict revenge backfired, as it turned out he so loved the fiery taste that he retailed the recipe at a chicken stand that was to have considerable local popularity.

Prince's Barbecue Chicken Shack had a few imitators, the most notable of which was started by Bolton Polk, a cook at Prince's who had a falling out with the boss. Under the name Colombo's and later Bolton's Hot Chicken and Fish, his restaurant achieved sufficient success to open a second Nashville branch in 2001. Lorrie Morgan and Sam Kershaw started a business called hotchickens.com, which, despite its name, was an actual physical location. Morgan's father was the country music great George Morgan, whose most famous song was "Candy Kisses," released in 1961. The singer had been accustomed to stopping by Bolton's on his way to and from the Grand Ole Opry and now he publicized hotchickens.com, but his daughter's enterprise failed nonetheless.

Nashville's international reputation for hot chicken was created by its mayor William Purcell, who publicized it indefatigably. In 2007, capping off his eight years of mayoral service, Purcell established the Music City Hot Chicken Festival. In that same year, 400 Degrees was opened by Aqui Simpson, followed by

Pepperfire in 2010, and, most successful of all, Hattie B's in 2012. Everyone has been careful to credit Prince's, and hot chicken history can be read (with some effort) as a story of racial collaboration, but Prince's invention required a set of white translators to be made comprehensible to an international public.

8 conviviality

We should look for someone to eat and drink with before looking for something to eat and drink, for dining alone is leading the life of a lion or wolf.

—EPICURUS

Having described the many ways in which food divides us, it is worth turning to how meals bring people together. The English word *commensality*, meaning dining in company, may seem like academic jargon, but it is a venerable term attested since the seventeenth century. Samuel Johnson defined commensality as "fellowship of the table; the custom of eating together." In 1826, an observer writing about members of the House of Commons being invited to dine with the Speaker imagined Dr. Johnson remarking, "Eating together promotes good will, Sir, commensality is benevolent." Yet companionable dining is so common that it has tended to pass unnoticed. One might say we have been practicing commensality all our lives without being aware of it.

Gustatory celebrations can be life-affirming expressions of family and community solidarity, accompanying occasions such as marriages, anniversaries, and school graduations. Meals with friends and relatives are often among our happiest memories. In *Antonia's Line,* a Dutch film from 1995, the life of the eponymous protagonist is punctuated by repasts with neighbors and family eaten outdoors at a long table. The plot is as much about the difficulties of life as about its accomplishments, but the latter are marked by commensality.

The Prophet Mohammed praised and recommended commensality: "Eat together and do not separate. Blessing is in society." The eleventh of the twelve Shi'ite Imams is supposed to have said, "When you sit at table with your brothers, sit long, for it is a time that is not counted against you as part of your lives."

Eating together takes on various forms, religious as well as worldly. In *The Religion of Java* (1960), one of the most notable anthropological studies of the twentieth century, Clifford Geertz identified the *slametan,* a short ceremonial meal, as the key to understanding Javanese life and worldview. A *slametan* is a carefully structured, understated response to life events, favorable or unfavorable, such as moving to a new house or the death of a family member. At the *slametan* nothing of substance is mentioned relating to what is being commemorated, no toasting or moment of silence, but rather the ritual of eating together itself creates a bond among the participants and between them and supernatural forces. Prepared by women, the food for the *slametan* is consumed by men sitting on the floor, eating with the fingers of the right hand and using banana leaves as plates.

Contemporary Western celebrations involve more ostentation than that presented by the *slametan.* Destination weddings, graduation parties, and major birthdays are usually accompanied by elaborate catering. By contrast, ordinary commensality is declining as family meals in Europe and North America have fallen apart in recent decades. The former custom of sitting down together every evening and exchanging news is recalled with wistful nostalgia, as evocative a relic of an analog world as typewriters, vinyl records, and "appointment TV."

Social scientists and the press routinely bemoan the isolated individualism of contemporary dining that sets aside the undoubted psychological benefits of sharing food with others. As meals have become hurried and utilitarian, the waning of commensality is assimilated to a crisis of community and the public sphere. While increasing loneliness can be attributed to technology and social disintegration, group dining has not actually been extinguished—it just doesn't take place at home. Before the Covid-19 pandemic, restaurants were immensely popular, and socializing over meals with friends was more common around the world than ever. This is not only because of the "foodie" wave, but because commensality creates, confirms, and extends relationships. Conversation at the table tells you about the other person, which is why the first instinct in wanting to get to know someone new is to share a meal.

Hollywood is aware of the relation between commensality and personality. Fabio Parasecoli, a food studies professor at New York University, studied blockbuster movies and found that virtually all included at least one scene of people preparing food or eating together. This is not because scriptwriters and directors are fond of gastronomy, but rather because they need to show character in a visual medium. For example, in *Pretty Woman* (1990), a romantic comedy that has nothing in its basic plot to do with food, Vivian Ward (Julia Roberts) has dinner with Edward Lewis (Richard Gere), a rapacious corporate executive who demonstrates his arrogant savoir faire by flawless gastronomic expertise. Before the intimidatingly elegant dinner, Vivian hastily learns some table etiquette, although she does not quite master how to pick up and extricate snails from their shells. The meal ends abruptly as the guests walk out, goaded and angered by Edward who gloats over having outsmarted them. Once he has humiliated his opponents, Edward loses interest in the gourmet charade. From this restaurant scene the viewer sees Edward's character and comes to know better the likeably awkward and plucky Vivian.

Preparing food can also be used to tell the viewer about character and social situations. *Twister,* a 1996 film about chasing tornados, is built on a central paradox that while this dangerous job is thought of as quintessentially male, Dr. Jo Harding is acknowledged to be unequaled as a spotter and tracker. In an early scene, the wives are cooking while the men are in another room trading stories. Harding, portrayed by Helen Hunt, is not welcomed by the women in the kitchen, who consider her not one of them, but she is also out of place with the guys. Food thus shows what this in-between character faces.

As the two movies exemplify, commensality does not always reinforce benevolence. Sharing and festivity can produce tension and dramatic conflict. Fights at dinner are frequent in novels and dramas, such as, for example, the violent altercation over Irish politics at Christmas dinner in James Joyce's *Portrait of the Artist as a Young Man.* Mundane, non-celebratory meals can degenerate as well. Jonathan Franzen's *The Corrections* gives a harrowing description of a boy refusing to eat his mashed rutabaga and being kept at the table for hours by his parents as he maintains his stubborn defiance.

And then there is the "Red Wedding" from George R. R. Martin's *Game of Thrones* series, an extreme example of deliberately derailed commensality at which almost all the Stark family guests are murdered. There is historical precedent, a banquet given in 750 A.D. to which the triumphant caliph of the Abbasid family invited princes of the deposed Umayyad dynasty. Billed as an occasion for reconciliation, the feast concluded with the clubbing to death of all the Umayyads except one, 'Abd al-Rahman ibn Mu'awiya, who escaped to establish the independent Emirate of Córdoba in Spain.

Commensality takes various forms, but in the contemporary developed world, restaurants are prominent venues. For several years before the pandemic, the average American family spent more money dining out than at home. Restaurants stand between the privacy of the family and the anonymity of cities and provide examples of the varieties of commensality.

Long before there were restaurants, taverns provided convivial companionship, though of a rowdy sort given the nature of their beverage offerings. Friendship, joking, and storytelling are encouraged by drinking together. Restaurants lend themselves to quieter and more private conversations. They have more extensive offerings and more varied settings than bars or cafés, and while their purpose is to serve food, they also encourage relationships and have profited from providing a place to talk with social, intellectual, or business associates. Restaurant commensality creates an opportunity to find out about other people. There are at least four kinds of socializing associated with restaurants: romance, friendship, celebration, and business.

Starting with the topic of romance, sexual attraction has always been structured by ways to meet potential intimate partners, from arranged marriages to mixers; from 1970s fern bars to online dating sites. In classical and medieval literature, couples did not tend to develop relationships over meals. In the *Inferno,* at the circle of the lustful, Francesca da Rimini tells Dante that her adulterous affair with her brother-in-law Paolo Malatesta originated from reading chivalric romances together; Tristan and Isolde were fatally attracted through a potion administered by mistake. During Jane Austen's era, promising matches might be encouraged by strategic seating at meals, but gatherings such as balls and chaperoned visits were better occasions for courtship.

Matchmaking and ceremonial visiting remain common in many parts of the world. Romance at restaurants requires sufficient relaxation of social rules to allow a young woman to be alone with a young man, and in northern Europe and the United States, this started to happen in the late nineteenth century. There is a scene in William Dean Howells's novel *A Modern Instance* (1882) in which Bartley Hubbard impresses the naive Marcia Gaylord with his ability to maneuver in a high social setting, nonchalantly ordering dinner in the dining room of Boston's Revere House Hotel and displaying "dazzling intelligence" with regard to selection. Restaurants were not sites for initiating relationships, but rather for following up an initial encounter. For a long time, dinner together was one of the first things a couple tried out in their early acquaintance, a recognized stage in the progress of intimacy.

If we proceed to the meals among friends, these involve a wider range of dining contexts than does romance. In many American small towns, old men meet for breakfast at a café, a

McDonald's, or a donut place to share news, well-worn stories, and random observations. Friendship is the reverse of courting because the point of getting together is not finding out about someone you have just contacted, but rather going over the same ground with characters you already know, and probably have known for years.

Camaraderie of this sort used to characterize adolescent socializing as well. The 1982 movie *Diner*, set in Baltimore in 1959, is about a group of male friends who have graduated from high school and are about to scatter to various places and take on different life roles. They frequently meet and eat together at a diner to discuss at length their often uncomfortable encounters with girls, but also, without quite realizing it, to put together memories against their imminent dispersal. A similar setting, here involving both young men and women, is the burger stand in *American Graffiti* (1973), another retrospective about a lost world. More recently, however, food has declined as a means to advance friendship, as Millennials and Generation Z conduct much of their lives online, and overscheduled teens do not have much time to hang out together in an unstructured setting. Fitting in ten minutes together at Starbucks is not the same.

A third well-known amicable meal type is what is covered by the dismissive term "ladies who lunch," originally a song from *Company*, Stephen Sondheim's musical of 1970. Female commensality goes back to just after the Civil War, the first time that middle-class women were able to have lunch at restaurants that attracted women of leisure who were shoppers as well as those working in offices and stores. Unlike elderly male breakfast cronies, they could be any adult age, partly because many women did not have a fixed schedule, and also because American women have tended to value friendship while men of the professional and executive ranks have been socialized to feel it's a waste of time.

Moving from friendship to festive events, it is obvious that celebrations are the oldest and best attested form of group dining. Roman banquets and Native American potlatches were collective feasts. Our society makes a point of observing family-oriented occasions such as anniversaries or birthdays. Feasts can be read as affirmations of social solidarity. Clubs, religious fellowships, guilds, and professional associations have at various times cemented common interests through celebratory dining.

Finally, meals provide business, professional, and political opportunities to talk face to face about sometimes vitally important affairs. Winston Churchill carefully planned the dinners he hosted for allies and rivals, including the meetings at Yalta and Potsdam with Stalin, Roosevelt, and Truman. In 1791, at the beginning of the French revolutionary terror, the restaurant Méot, whose menu offered more than 250 choices, was a gathering place for judges and members of the revolutionary committees such as Danton and Robespierre who, over dinner, drew up lists of those to be guillotined in subsequent days.

In order to use a restaurant to devise less bloodthirsty schemes, to make contacts and connections, you need to take meals there repeatedly and predictably, proving you are in the game. As Al Sharpton said of Sylvia's in Harlem: "You had to show up from time to time or else people thought you had retired." High society has always functioned this way—to be a favored courtier in the reign of Louis XIV required attending at the palace of Versailles. No matter how imposing your provincial chateau, you were unimportant if you resided there continuously.

Within the rarefied circle of a court or a noble household, there might be a feverish need to prove one's position, but aristocratic socializing did not require flattering attention from the masses. The restaurant, however, reflects the aspirations of the haute bourgeoisie in the nineteenth century, whose status was rooted in wealth, not in birth, titles, or land. Members of this newly powerful group entertained on a level of splendor to rival and even surpass that of the nobility, but public notice was important. Most businesspeople want discretion and clubbiness at their favorite restaurants, but they also need exposure. The restaurant benefits its inner circle of regulars, but it also has to provide an audience for them.

After the Civil War, American wealth and status were less stable than for the noble families of Europe. The Gilded Age was dominated by great fortunes accumulated through industry, but by the 1890s and accelerating after the First World War, restaurants also staged a new kind of social distinction. The manufacturing and financial elite was supplemented by a faster crowd of movie stars, international playboys, sports notables, even the more presentable sort of criminals. Because Prohibition thinned the ranks of elegant restaurants, night clubs such as the Cotton Club in Harlem or El Morocco and the Stork Club in midtown Manhattan replaced them as places to be seen—what the gossip columnist Walter Winchell referred to as "watering holes."

Today successful people in most fields no longer regard lunch as a transactional opportunity. LinkedIn and staged networking events appear more important and time-efficient than midday dining. Julia Phillips's autobiography in 1991 about the movie industry was titled *You'll Never Eat Lunch in This Town Again,* and while there are still celebrity haunts in Los Angeles, the entertainment business no longer requires constant midday dining out. Before the Covid-19 epidemic, New York book publishing notables still embraced lunch at restaurants such as Michael's and Union Square Café, where agents, authors, and publishers could gossip or work out agreements, but deal-making in banking or real estate had already ceased to take place over meals.

Commensality is both warm-heartedly egalitarian and hierarchical. Although it is usually presented as bringing people together to share food and reinforce emotional connections, people can also be assembled to demonstrate power and to underline differences in status. Part of the function of banquets has been to exhibit, even celebrate, inequality.

At pre-modern celebrations, not everybody got to enjoy the same delicacies. Twenty-five hundred guests attended a banquet at York following the enthronement of George Neville as archbishop in 1465, seated at tables spread out over several rooms of the castle of Cawood. A high table, set at one end of the principal hall, was occupied by bishops, dukes, and earls. Six other tables accommodated important monastic officials and the lesser nobility, and then at increasing distance were placed members of the York cathedral chapter, officials of the city of York, men of law and other lay functionaries, and young esquires of the royal court. Beyond the great hall were further chambers seating ladies of prominence, lesser gentlemen and their wives, and finally a gallery for the servants of the various guests. Each table got a different set of courses, with a greater number being provided for the higher-rated ones.

At a series of wedding dinners in Florence in June 1469, the guests at the marriage of Lorenzo de' Medici and Clarice degl' Orsini were arranged not by status but according to a more complicated sociology in which hierarchy yielded some ground to staging. The bride and fifty of her girlfriends dined in the garden of the Medici Palace. Leading Florentine citizens sat in the courtyard; young men were served on the first floor *sala* and the older women were upstairs on a balcony. The girls were favored because of their beauty rather than their rank. Visible to all, they were protected by their separate space although intermittently available to talk to when, for example, they went through the courtyard out into the street to dance.

Sometimes a carefully planned event broke down and gate-crashing resulted in excess and subverted hierarchy. The complexity of pulling off simultaneously a public fête and a more *soigné* private meal always creates logistical problems. The boy king Henry VI of England was crowned twice, once at Westminster in 1429 at the age of seven, and then two years later in Paris, as the English were starting to lose the Hundred Years' War to the French. The Parisian coronation was a catering disaster. Members of the populace forced their way into the hall where the feast was being prepared, eating what had been already set out, stealing salt cellars and other portable table-service items, and resisting all attempts to move them to make way for the invited members of the *parlement,* university faculty, merchant officials, and other urban dignitaries who were forced to share the chaotic revels with their social inferiors.

Plans miscarried at the inaugural party on March 6, 1865, for what was supposed to be Abraham Lincoln's second presidential term. The menu included fifty-three items, more than half of them desserts: cakes, tarts, creams, ice creams, and fruit ices. Three hundred people were invited to attend the event standing (only the most select of the company actually sat down to dine), but five thousand crammed into the West Wing of the White House. According to the *New York Times,* "The crush which followed can better be imagined than depicted . . . in less than an hour the table was a wreck . . . a demolition in a twinkling of an eye of all the confectioner's handiwork . . . as much was wasted as was eaten, and however much there may have been provided, more than half the guests went supperless."

Even when arrangements unfolded efficiently, there were distinctions among the guests, but that was the meaning of the event that amounted, like life itself, to a combination of regimentation and disarray. One was supposed to be grateful just to have been invited. To this day in many societies, who sits down, who eats what food, and in what order are informally but consistently regulated. Eating together reflects and celebrates social connections, but it also demonstrates divisions based on status, gender, and ethnicity that we have already seen. The global contexts and circumstances of our meals are as important as what we actually consume. The next chapter looks at the wider implications of those meals for the intimidating future of our world, where they come from, and what are their social and environmental costs.

9 food and the present crises

. . . the intellectual puzzle of our time: what lies at the root of pervasive inaction, wishful thinking, and denial?

—ELKE WEBER

This concluding chapter considers the current situation and the future of food and was written and revised during the first eight months of the Covid-19 pandemic. It reflects the sudden intrusion of a crisis that makes thoughts about the future more urgent. As is true with so many aspects of life, the pandemic has not so much created new situations as accelerated trends already under way, bringing unpredictability and fragility into the foreground of previously comfortable lives. Some of this revelation of a more dangerous situation is dramatic and terrible, as with the fires and storms that threaten the western and southern United States, but no less revolutionary are small-scale novelties—the first time most people in well-off countries ever waited in line to get into a grocery store or experienced restriction of their physical movement and social contacts. As the environmental historian Bill McKibben put it, most people in the Western world have taken food and water for granted—one comes from a store, the other from a tap—but physical reality does not always bend to our will or assumptions.

What formerly were phenomena of the distant past, of interest only to historians—the influenza epidemic of 1918, or cholera in the nineteenth century—became suddenly relevant. Even the impact and aftershocks of the apocalyptic-scale Black Death of

1348–1349, with a mortality rate of over ninety percent of those affected, offers parallels to such now-familiar phenomena as blame-shifting, vicious conspiracy theories, social rebellion, and extremes of hedonist and pious behavior.

Crises test and mislead, but they also concentrate the mind, freeing it from the illusions and preoccupations of comfortable and absorbing everyday life. It is obvious that a global problem has met different responses. Countries like South Korea and Taiwan that acted quickly and competently when the pandemic started in the winter of 2020 were able to ward it off, while those that embraced delay and denial were devastated. The coronavirus has made it harder to ignore the inequities of how our world, including its food supply and distribution, actually works. The reality hasn't changed; it was always there, hidden under layers of distraction and deliberate obfuscation, but then suddenly and somehow surprisingly visible, much as the radical decrease in driving, air travel, and factory production scoured the air temporarily so that mountains long-hidden by pollution were visible. Twitter posts from cities in Punjab marveled at the startling beauty of the snow-capped Himalayas, which could be seen for the first time in three decades. In Nairobi, many residents were shocked to discover that Mount Kenya looms above their city. It has become similarly clearer where our food comes from, how it gets to us, and what the effects of its production, consumption, and disposal are on workers and the environment.

The damaging aspects of the food supply chain were never a great secret. For years science and food writers have presented reliable, accessible information about the dangers of global food production. Dependence on overseas factories and farms maximizes profits because of cheap foreign labor. Boasts about "efficiencies" such as just-in-time inventory or offshoring ignored issues related to control over production and backups for disruption. In a world of accentuated unpredictability related to disease, war, politics, and climate disasters, managers have belatedly rediscovered resilience and reliability, what is referred to as cautious "just in case" management.

Notwithstanding how much is still unknown about the long-term consequences of the pandemic, we can ask which innovations might work to draw humanity back from the precipice of mass destruction from not only the immediate effects of pestilence but the long-term but now accelerating alteration of nature. Looking at climate change and disease control, let's consider the promises and possible drawbacks of technologies and ideas advanced to ameliorate our pressing problems.

It is expected that another 1.7 billion people will be added to the world's population by 2050. Accompanying demographic and economic growth are changes in diet, such as increased meat consumption in rapidly developing countries, that put further pressure on the food system. The mantra of increased production and efficiency still dominates official and corporate discourse. Insofar as ecological considerations are accommodated, they are fit into a "trade-offs" model. Dam-building or deforestation are thus analyzed according to a cost-benefit scheme, forest destruction but more cattle; displacement of population and widespread environmental degradation but more electricity. The cumulative price of this unsustainable devastation in the name of economic growth is increasingly obvious. Treating sustainability as negotiable and capable of being compromised indefinitely will no longer work, if it ever did.

Even when environmental urgency intrudes itself on decision-making, academics and policymakers almost fatuously assume the good will of political leaders and avoid looking at the actions of those who actually runs things now. It should not come as surprising news that not all leaders prioritize science, relieving suffering, or environmental stewardship. Whatever recommendations researchers make to relieve global problems related to food and the environment, their implementation depends on the priorities of the political elites.

It is insufficient to exalt science as the just determinative given the poor record of expertise in managing the planet over the previous one or two centuries. Yesterday's technological breakthrough has a way of becoming today's crisis, and not just with obvious horrors like the atomic bomb. Championed by international agencies, what was dubbed the "Green Revolution" increased food production substantially in the half century between 1962 and 2012. The combination of high-yield seeds, mechanical irrigation, and intensive fertilization improved agricultural productivity, especially for basic cereals. That revolution's corollaries, however, the massive water projects and inputs of pesticides and fertilizers, cannot be perpetuated as they have accelerated water depletion, soil degradation, and biodiversity decline.

True, there is an after-the-fact ecological justification for the Green Revolution, because agricultural yield was tripled using only thirty percent more land, thereby, in theory, saving millions of undeveloped acres from exploitation. But in reality, pristine lands were decimated for reasons unconnected to the struggle against starvation. Trees were cut down to make money from livestock ranching, mining, urban expansion, and tourism.

Asserting the overriding necessity to feed the planet has been an excuse to exalt technocratic intervention. It serves to denigrate efforts to dismantle unsustainable agriculture by typifying such plans as naive or unworkable while ignoring the damage presently being done to climate, water, food systems, and other basic factors on which human survival depends.

How will we feed the planet in the future, especially if traditional technological solutions involving chemicals, dams, or land clearance have reached their limits? The international agency charged with assuring an adequate food supply is the United Nations' Food and Agriculture Organization (FAO). Since its inception in 1945, the FAO's mission has been to alleviate hunger by improving agricultural productivity. Initially set up to deal with postwar food crises, the FAO experienced its golden age in terms of prestige and budget during the 1950s and 1960s, when large amounts of money were made available for development and technology that radically improved crop yields.

Today, although belatedly concerned with sustainability, the FAO and other global food agencies remain committed, understandably, to a feed-the-planet model. In 2014 the FAO identified what it called a "confluence of pressures" on agriculture: 1) malnutrition caused by poverty and inequality; 2) inadequate diets joined with unsustainable consumption patterns; 3) land scarcity and soil degradation; 4) water depletion and pollution; 5) extinction and declining biodiversity; 6) climate change; and 7) lack of invest-ment in agricultural research.

Having identified seven problems, the FAO document then announces, "Five Principles of Sustainable Agriculture." These are worth examining because they involve policy ideas imple-mented in the real world. The FAO reiterates the old develop-mental model although acknowledging global victims and mixing in some unlikely hopes. The first principle is that improving efficiency in the exploitation of resources, not just crop yield, is critical to sustainable agriculture. This recognizes that maximiz-ing production has to consider the startlingly inefficient use of water and profligate application of mineral fertilizer. Almost three-quarters of the water used by human beings goes to agriculture. Fertilizer is similarly wasted; the fertilizer "uptake efficiency" for rice in China, for example, is about twenty-seven percent, meaning that seventy-three percent shows up as nitrate contamination of water. And to make that mostly useless fertilizer requires immense amounts of energy, representing an additional contribution to greenhouse gases. More efficient use of resources would mean tending the soil, what is called "regenerative farm-ing," adding nitrogen the old-fashioned way. Legumes and trees would be integrated into cropping as, in effect, "green manure."

The second principle expresses concern about the survival of rural agricultural communities that account for considerably more than half of the impoverished population of the world. It recommends compensation for conservation of green resources (what are called "payment schemes for environmental services"), meaning that farmers should be indemnified for not destroying endangered ecosystems.

This may be generally commendable, but the FAO is in effect blaming the problem on its victims. Traditional agriculture is frequently (and often cynically) numbered among the enemies of sustainability, the finger pointing at what is inaccurately termed "slash-and-burn" cultivation, clearing forest land and then moving on after a few years when the soil's nutrients have been depleted. The very term "slash and burn" misleadingly implies massive environmental destruction, but its traditional practitioners have been quite aware of how to manage cultivation sustainably. In the 1950s, Harold Conklin showed that the Hanunoo in the Philippines practiced a complex and successful form of shifting agriculture and land conservation. The Hanunoo at that time periodically cleared land for gardens of dazzling biodiversity and moved among different places in rotation to allow nutrients to be replenished. Massive global deforestation is taking place not because of the practices of indigenous people but through the agency of corporations enabled by governments, such as those of Indonesia, Brazil, or the Congo. The scale of mechanical destruction for timber operations, mining, dam-building, road construction, and agricultural land clearance is much greater than anything attributable to poor, technologically backward farmers.

FAO principle three, to ensure healthy lives and to promote well-being, is merely hortatory. Suffice it to say that the FAO itself acknowledges that to connect the efficiencies that the first and second principles represent with the issues of equity and social conservation recognized by principle three "presents major challenges."

The fourth principle conveys a realistic hope that if we stop abusing the earth, it will heal itself. As shown during the involuntary tranquility of the early pandemic, nature has surprising powers of recuperation. If after just a couple of months the water in Venetian canals ran clear, who knows what might happen if some serious remedies were put into long-term effect? That people and communities are similarly resilient, as the FAO claims, is less likely. Uprooted from their homes, farms, food customs, and points of orientation, migrants cannot readily get back what they have lost.

Finally, the fifth principle, which closely resembles the second, states that sustainability requires direct action to protect natural resources. Even more than with the other principles, good intentions go against the reality of ineffective and unethical governments and a global economy whose powerful actors are heavily invested in unsustainable practices. While most nations (with some lamentable exceptions) have signed on to international agreements such as the Convention on Biodiversity or the Paris Climate Agreement, it will require more than such gestures, especially a serious corporate buy-in, for the treaties to have much effect.

One of the reasons sustainability is hard to put into practice is that food production has become a lucrative investment. The movement of money is a key factor in the globalization of food. Anticipating shortages and wanting to control trade in agricultural products, China, Persian Gulf sovereign wealth funds, and private entities like investment banks have bought resources, especially in Africa, which has the largest amount of "vacant" arable land in the world and where governments have been easy to influence. Most of what is acquired is not actually vacant in the sense of its being empty wilderness. Rather it is occupied by people who do not count, according to the planning priorities of companies, international agencies, or states. Land held in common and used for subsistence agriculture and herding is being placed under private ownership. Ordering land into registered parcels sounds like an efficiency reform, but it has the effect of seizing and privatizing formerly open, available resources. The newly created property is being monetized and globalized, turned into contract agriculture by which farmers grow export crops like those string beans in Burkina Faso.

According to measurements set by international agencies like the World Trade Organization or the International Monetary Fund, export agriculture looks as if it assists local economies, but in reality it benefits relatively few actors such as government officials who receive money for the transactions and entrepreneurs who can take advantage of crop production. The losers, who are vastly more numerous, are those who were previously growing their own food or tending their own animals. Dispossessed by land grabs as well as climate shifts, these former small proprietors are now among the refugees who further swell the dysfunctional cities of the Global South or who try to reach Europe or the United States. Some cities are approaching the point of collapse. Karachi has twenty million inhabitants. Its increasing summer temperatures, now sometimes above 110 degrees, and a longer and wilder monsoon season of rains and flooding are rendering it close to uninhabitable.

The first two sentences of a *New York Times Magazine* article titled "Refugees from the Earth" by Abrahm Lustgarten summarize a grim current and an even worse future situation: "New research suggests that climate change will cause humans to move across the planet at an unprecedented, destabilizing scale. For many, the great climate migration has already begun." In much of Guatemala, for example, rainfall is projected to decrease by seventy percent over the next fifty years, and in its north-central province of Alta Verapaz, the rice yield is expected by 2070 to have declined by one-third. Already hundreds of thousands of Guatemalans have fled northward, to Mexico and the United States.

Crises involving hunger and migration are not caused exclusively by meteorological events, but stem also from ideologies and practices put into effect since 1980. The dismantling of protectionism and the free circulation of investment meant that farmers everywhere were increasingly at the mercy of volatile global markets. In keeping with neoliberalism (reducing or eliminating government intervention in the name of the free market), deregulation and intensified economic competition have lessened self-sufficiency for rural people. These changes have monetized what were formerly matters of local supply and demand. Market logic and globalization have made the structure of interconnection more susceptible to the sort of disruption the Covid-19 pandemic produced.

Given the intellectual and political weakness displayed by policymakers, we can only hope that paradoxically science might release us from the bind its progress has placed us in. And there is some reason for optimism. Renewable energy sources are becoming cheaper and more efficient rapidly, having already contributed to coal's decline and likely next to reverse expansion of the use of natural gas. Artificial intelligence is being applied to irrigation; cultivar biodiversity is being restored. The oceans are increasingly depleted and climate change is making them less hospitable to many species, but ecologically virtuous systems of fish farming are being successfully developed.

I will discuss two innovations that have received considerable media notice: genetically modified organisms (GMOs) and alternatives to meat based on plants or on laboratory-grown ingredients. These illustrate the interaction of cultural attitudes and scientific developments.

GMOs are intended as engineered solutions to the problems of climate change such as drought, and the environmental impact of toxic agricultural inputs such as artificial fertilizer, herbicides, and pesticides. Modified seeds produce plants that need less water, can survive heat, and are resistant to insects and blights. Additionally, genetic alteration is supposed to make the plant more nutritious. GMOs differ from conventional crossbreeding because they involve gene combinations that do not occur in nature by using DNA from another organism, which might be a plant, animal, virus, or bacterium. GMO engineering has been applied to strengthen corn, soy, canola, alfalfa, and sugar beets. In the United States over ninety percent of the harvest of these basic crops has been genetically manipulated.

GMOs have led to modest increases in production, but these come with drawbacks that fall into several categories: claims not borne out by reality, the threat of unforeseen and irreversible damage to species integrity, and unacceptable trade-offs affecting the environment. Most importantly, the shift to GMO crops has not brought about a decrease in the use of chemicals. Rather than being pest- or weed-resistant, GMO varieties turn out to be better at tolerating pesticides and herbicides. The new organisms can withstand more chemical inputs, so in fact the quantity of damaging chemicals used in agriculture has increased. The accelerated destruction of natural soil nutrients and the pollution of ground and river water are the perverse outcomes of what looks like success by the business-as-usual metric of maximizing yield. Furthermore, consolidation of the industries controlling seeds and agriculture-related chemicals increases the orientation toward augmenting rather than decreasing pesticide and herbicide use. Monsanto (acquired recently by Bayer) makes the weed killer Roundup. Bayer agreed in June 2020 to pay out $10 billion to settle claims that the pesticide caused cancer, and yet it is still on the market and used everywhere.

On the bright side, the worst-case, Jurassic Park scenario for GMOs has not materialized. Poisoning of consumers and damage to established breeds have also been avoided so far. In 2016, 103 Nobel laureates published a statement denouncing the environmental activists of Greenpeace for their opposition to GMOs. The laureates expatiated more on what might be called non-costs rather than on actual benefits. They argued that GMOs did no apparent direct damage to human health or existing plant species and this was taken to mean that their use was good. Among the most important but only tangentially discussed effects of GMOs is that most applications have been for First World export crops such as corn, soybeans, and cotton, while crops that farmers cultivate in developing countries are neglected—things like yams, cassava, or millet.

Another promising but not yet proven innovation is an alternative to meat from animals. There are two paths of development, one based on plants selected, flavored, and textured to resemble meat, and the other the laboratory-based cultivation of proteins, a kind of artificial rather than imitation meat. One or both of these forms of engineering, it is hoped, will result in something whose production imposes minimal damage on the natural world, yet in taste is indistinguishable from meat.

Raising domestic animals is among the leading contributors to environmental crises. Creating new pastures is the main motivation for deforestation in South America. Concentrated animal feeding operations crowd animals together for maximum efficiency, requiring administration of large quantities of antibiotics and releasing huge amounts of methane and ammonia. The meat-to-plant ratio of impact on the water supply is particularly impressive. It takes five times as much water to produce a kilogram of beef than a kilogram of wheat.

Livestock concentration creates opportunities for pathogens both because of the poor health of the animals and because crowding allows a virus or bacteria to replicate faster, since a new host is so close and has the same genetic makeup as the previous victim. While the so-called wet markets of China are notorious breeding grounds for several international viruses, inadequately regulated factory farming conditions in the United States are comparably dangerous.

Meat consumption leveled off in Europe long ago, but it has grown rapidly in China and in developing countries whose citizens until recently were only rarely able to afford meat. In 1991, China's annual per capita appetite for meat was about twenty kilograms. By 2002 it had doubled, and although the acceleration in recent years is less, the number has risen to between fifty and sixty kilograms, pork and poultry primarily. Given the global demand for beef, chicken, and pork and their damaging environmental consequences, mass acceptance of plant-based or laboratory products that effectively mimic the taste, texture, and even the juice produced by cooking meat would considerably ameliorate damage to the air, water, soil, and climate of our beleaguered planet.

Products meant to imitate meat have a long history. Vegetarian restaurants used to feature "nut cutlet," but although crushed nuts could be shaped and colored, the result did not taste like meat. Chinese cooks can turn tofu into dishes that more effectively imitate duck and other forms of poultry and meat. The rise in meat consumption, however, shows that given funds and opportunity, consumers will choose real duck over the cleverest mock version.

Plant-based meat brands such as Beyond Burger or Impossible Burger have achieved success in attracting consumers. Their selling point cannot be natural, healthful ingredients, since they rely on sodium and other enhancements to imitate the flavor, texture, and color of meat. Nor is their price dramatically lower than that of animal meat, although in the future, given both the increasing problems of meat processing and the scalability of plant-based products, this should change. The main advantage of Impossible Burger and the like is that the ratio of land that can be figured as necessary to raise equivalent amounts of animal versus plant-based meat is on the order of 10 to 1.

As with GMOs, plant-based meat has been oversold. Restaurants' reorder rates have been disappointing and even though Burger King and other chains have adopted plant-based options, this may be a public relations gesture, producing reputational dividends rather than high sales figures. The consumer might be glad to know there is a plant-based option, even as he or she orders a beefburger.

There are also new developments in making artificial meat using animal muscle tissue. Cell-cultured products are just getting to the marketable stage, so it is too early to tell if they can reproduce the taste and mouthfeel of meat better than plant-based varieties can. This is particularly significant for eventually going beyond just ground meat. An advantage of animal over plant cells is that they can more effectively replicate the qualities of meat that is not chopped up, so lab-meat holds the promise of greater variety and more enthusiastic consumer acceptance. In December 2020, lab-grown chicken was approved for sale, first in Singapore.

The paradox of these alternative meat ventures is that they are supported for environmental reasons by the same people who oppose GMOs and junk food laden with chemical ingredients. Both plant-based and cell-cultured meat are highly processed and clearly artificial. In these respects, they evoke twentieth-century scenarios of a dystopian future. Most of the denizens of Aldous

Huxley's *Brave New World* (1932) are content with vitamin-enriched artificial beef. In George Orwell's *1984* (published in 1949), what passes for food is at best tasteless, reflecting the author's experience of wartime and postwar rationing and the irritatingly cheerful efforts of the British government to claim that dubious products such as the South African canned *snoeck*, resembling barracuda, could be rendered palatable. Susan Cooper's chapter on British food and housekeeping in a collection of essays, *The Age of Austerity* (1945–1951), is titled "Snoeck Piquante." During a frightful period when bread was rationed, and even dried eggs and powdered milk were scarce, the authorities tried to persuade people to eat whale meat and snoeck, with no success, showing there are certain things even desperation cannot make attractive.

In speculative fiction only the privileged or a few stubborn if hapless rebels remember how food is supposed to taste. The overpopulated world of the movie *Soylent Green* (1973), directed by Richard Fleischer and starring Charlton Heston, does have strawberry jam, but only for an extraordinarily high price. The normal subsistence food, from which the movie gets its title, is revealed to be made using human corpses. Julia, in George Orwell's *1984*, enjoys "proper white bread," along with sugar, coffee, and jam. On Indian reservations, as depicted in *Brave New World*, wild rabbits, tortillas, and corn are available instead of the standard carotene sandwiches.

Current versions of technologically engineered food seem better than what twentieth-century writers expected, but alternative meat is creating political and cultural conflicts because of the suspicion that the elite will impose a lower standard on the masses and reserve for itself the first-class version. In this case only high-income families will be able to afford real meat. Like guns and incandescent lightbulbs, red meat has become something privileged liberals supposedly want to take away from ordinary people in the name of safety or the environment. In a tweet on October 23, 2020, Clay Higgins, a Republican U.S. representative from Louisiana, reported that his clairvoyant wife had dreamed that federal agents were in their home seizing guns, knives, stored water, and "unauthorized foods." "What happened to our freedom?" his wife asked upon waking. Comments to the tweet asked what was meant by unauthorized foods, with speculation centering on beef, game, or maybe packaged snacks like Cheetos.

What is particularly enraging, according to such scenarios, is that the wealthy have no intention of living by the rules any more than they plan to send their children to public high schools. Alternatively, and even more objectionable, is that some liberals *do* sanctimoniously accept things like artificial meat and water-conserving toilets, because they have become corrupted by cultural decay. If meat-eating is gendered male, advocates of alternative meat appear to be opening up yet another front against masculinity. The resentment is directed toward feminist vegetarians but ever more against young urban sophisticates of ambiguous sexuality—men who use moisturizer and order avocado toast along with their artificial burger.

The ominous science fiction of the twentieth century seems to predict some of the scenarios unfolding in the twenty-first. Some of this is simply the replacement of one set of doomsday instigators with another: climate change instead of nuclear war. The two greatest current worries, climate change and pestilence, seem to differ in that the first seems modern while disease is perennial. Climate change is not exactly new either, however. Historical research is showing that climate shifts created crises from the era of the Roman Empire to the increasing agricultural productivity in Europe beginning in the ninth century. It is our perception of what is happening and the increased speed of dangerous trends that is now different because of globalization and modern communications. What the Covid-19 epidemic and climate change have in common is that they have moved faster and more dangerously than even scientists predicted.

The Covid-19 pandemic temporarily diverted attention from the climate problem but also showed it to be even more urgent. Perhaps the disease onslaught will clear the way for radical change, because like it or not, things are shifting rapidly beyond what in 2019 was considered unalterable circumstance. The coronavirus proved to be a game-changer rather than an interruption.

Although not growing with the speed of a global epidemic, climate change has overtaken the world relatively quickly, especially in terms of public awareness. Recent evidence has not only validated the warming trend but found that it is escalating with more speed than originally forecast. Predictions and models of warming go back to 1973, but the beginning of a widespread sense of impending crisis may be dated to Al Gore's movie *An Inconvenient Truth* from 2006. It was anticipated by the classic 1961 film *The Day the Earth Caught Fire,* in which a sudden doomsday warming of the earth is caused by nuclear testing altering its orbit; the real-world change taking place inexorably today is the result not of atomic explosions but of everyday technologies.

The message of *An Inconvenient Truth* was mocked by fossil fuel companies and right-wing commentators. Now, very late in the day, scientific data and concerned investors are altering business attitudes. Climate change acceleration mirrors the shift from theoretical to here-and-now with regard to epidemic disease. The Covid-19 pandemic was predicted before bursting on the scene in China at the end of 2019. The Ebola virus had killed thousands in Africa; Zika hit Brazil; and SARS damaged China. Because these diseases did not reach Europe or North America, virus worries were in those areas considered just another form of background noise until the fatal year 2020.

The effects of climate change are being experienced across the earth and are damaging food cultivation and supply, a situation that will get worse. Despite some favorable paradoxes (a new wine industry in Denmark, for instance), global warming creates chronic droughts as well as increasingly violent and frequent storms. It imposes stress on plants and soil and more quickly evaporates water used for irrigation. Even in minimally affected New England, climate change has already made it impossible for salmon to live in the Connecticut River, contributed to the collapse of the cod industry, given Maine for the time being a bounty of lobsters displaced from Connecticut and Rhode Island water, and now threatens commercial profits from cranberries, clams, and sugar maples.

When climate disasters were associated with desertification in what Westerners considered remote and benighted regions such as sub-Saharan Africa, they tended to be relegated to the category of random events. On the other hand, fires in California and Australia are spectacular proof of immediacy for the previously complacent, even if the impact has not yet extended to the food supply. The pandemic too functions as a jolting lesson in the fragility of our lives and the systems they are built on. It also has affected food practices from agricultural labor shortages to the permanent closure of restaurants.

The coronavirus had contradictory short-term effects. It caused a temporary although dramatic slowdown in consumption, petroleum use, and pollution. More food was cooked at home, which is in general healthier than dining out, and simple products like beans were rediscovered. At the same time, canned, frozen, and convenience products saw a spurt in sales after years of decline. Maybe the newest celebrity chef turns out to be Chef Boy-ar-dee.

Declining income and business closures may wipe out the farm-to-table paradigm, which depends on better quality but higher priced goods. The customers for small farms with traditional methods were largely restaurants, and even those that survive will have trouble selling to consumers in an economy with less dining out. On the other hand, European governments are mandating that homegrown agricultural products replace imports, and the xenophobic agenda behind such demands may yield to a more constructive understanding of the virtues of small-scale, local farming.

Current events are creating a crisis for *homo economicus,* the human being conceived as reducible to a unit of economic productivity and an inexhaustible desire for things. Is economic activity more important than controlling a disease? Does it outweigh environmental degradation? Why, even now, are people not sufficiently scared of the effects of climate change? Can the gross national product continue to increase in the face of persistent illness and increased climate-related adversity? These questions are now at the center of American, Brazilian, Russian, and British political divisions. As I have argued throughout this book, the importance of food is determined not solely by scientific evidence or cost-benefit calculations but by cultural assumptions and public opinion.

Assumptions and outlook are affected by expertise but also by demagoguery. The experts have failed on a number of issues, from overconfidence in large-scale agriculture to free-market justifications for corporate rapacity. The flawed agenda set by the best and the brightest has given rise to anger and fear that not only undermines science but promotes conspiracies and nostrums at odds with basic facts.

What should we do? In an article about how to get people to treat climate change with appropriate urgency, Elke U. Weber quotes Amory Lovins's succinct recommendation:

> Be neither an optimist nor a pessimist. Both are different forms of fatalism. Instead, practice what I call *applied hope:* believe our world and the causes you care about can get better, and work to make them so.

How to do this is a question for all of us but hardly an easy determination. In terms of food matters, if I were forced to choose between what one culinary historian, Ken Albala, calls "culinary

Luddism"—rejecting processing and making everything your-self—and what another, Rachel Laudan, refers to as "culinary mod-ernism" (embracing processed and factory-produced food), my heart would be Luddite. But then again, my stomach and the ev-eryday behavior it dictates seem determined to live by modernism. There will be a set of intermediate paths between Luddism and modernism, but they will not amount to solutions in the sense of resolving threats. Rather, they are accommodations to what prom-ises to be a constrained if just maybe rejuvenating life in the future.

bibliography

Assael, Brenda. *The London Restaurant, 1840–1914* (Oxford: Oxford University Press, 2018).

Appadurai, Anthony. *Modernity at Large* (Minneapolis: University of Minnesota Press, 1996).

Benito i Monclús, Pere, ed. *Crisis alimentarias en la Edad Media: Modelos, explicaciones y representaciones* (Llcida: Milenio, 2013).

Bennett, Judith M. *A Medieval Life: Cecilia Penifader of Brigstock, ca. 1295–1344*, 2nd ed. (Philadelphia: University of Pennsylvania Press, 2020).

Bhutto, Fatima. "Pakistan's Most Terrifying Adversary Is Climate Change," *New York Times,* September 27, 2020, https://www.nytimes.com/2020/09/27/opinion/pakistan-climate-change.html.

Brumberg-Kraus, Jonathan. *Gastronomic Judaism as Culinary Midrash* (Lanham, Md.: Rowman and Littlefield, 2018).

Bynum, Caroline. *Holy Feast, Holy Fast: The Religious Significance of Food to Medieval Women* (Berkeley and Los Angeles: University of California Press, 1987).

Campanini, Antonella. *Food Cultures in Medieval Europe,* trans. Leah M. Ashe (Brussels: Peter Lang, 2019).

Chang, David, and Gabe Ulla. *Eat a Peach* (New York: Penguin, 2020).

Chiquart. *Du fait de cuisine: On Cookery of Master Chiquart (1420),* ed. and trans. Terence Scully (Tempe: Arizona Center for Medieval and Renaissance Studies, 2010).

Condé, Maryse. *Of Morsels and Marvels,* trans. Richard Philcox (Kolkata: Seagull Books, 2015).

Dirks, Robert. *Food in the Gilded Ages: What Ordinary Americans Ate* (Lanham, Md.: Rowman and Littlefield, 2016).

Edge, John T. *The Potlikker Papers: A Food History of the Modern South* (New York: Penguin, 2017).

Finn, S. Margo. *Discriminating Taste: How Class Anxiety Created the American Food Revolution* (New Brunswick: Rutgers University Press, 2017).

The Food Lovers' Anthology (Oxford: Bodleian Library, 2014).

Friedman, Andrew. *Chefs, Drugs, and Rock and Roll: How Food Lovers, Free Spirits, Misfits, and Wanderers Created a New American Profession* (New York: HarperCollins, 2018).

Geertz, Clifford. *The Religion of Java* (Glencoe, Ill.: Free Press, 1960).

Goldstein, Joyce. *Inside the California Food Revolution: Thirty Years That Changed Our Culinary Consciousness* (Berkeley and Los Angeles: University of California Press, 2013).

Halawa, Mateusz, and Fabio Parasecoli. "Eating and Drinking in Global Brooklyn," *Food, Culture and Society* 22 (2019), 387–406.

Hall, Kim P. "Culinary Spaces, Colonial Spaces: The Gendering of Sugar in the Seventeenth Century," in *Feminist Readings of Early Modern Culture: Emerging Subjects,* ed. Valerie Traub et al. (Cambridge: Cambridge University Press, 1996), pp. 168–190.

Harris, Jessica B. *Beyond Gumbo: Creole Fusion Food from the Atlantic Rim* (New York: Simon and Schuster, 2003).

Harris, Jessica B. *High on the Hog: A Culinary Journey from Africa to America* (New York: Bloomsbury, 2011).

Inness, Sherrie A. *Dinner Roles: American Women and Culinary Culture* (Iowa City: University of Iowa Press, 2001).

Kaufman, Frederick. *Bet the Farm: How Food Stopped Being Food* (New York: John Wiley and Sons, 2012).

Kunze, Rui. "Stakes of Authentic Culinary Experience: Food Writing of Tang Lusun and Wang Zengqi," *Ex-position* 43 (June 2020), 109–135.

Lapham's Quarterly, vol. 4, no. 3 (2011). Issue devoted to food.

Lappé, Frances. *Diet for a Small Planet* (New York: Ballantine, 1971).

Lorr, Benjamin. *The Secret Life of Groceries: The Dark Side of the American Supermarket* (New York: Penguin, 2020).

Lustgarten, Abrahm. "Refugees from the Earth," *New York Times Magazine,* July 26, 2020, pp. 8–23, 43–45.

Mario, Thomas. *The Playboy Gourmet* (Secaucus, N.J.: Castle Books, 1977).

Martinus of Como. *The Art of Cooking: The First Modern Cookery Book,* ed. Luigi Ballerini et al. (Berkeley and Los Angeles: University of California Press, 2005).

McAllister, Ward. *Society as I Have Found It* (New York: Cassell, 1890).

McCarron, Meghan, "The Chefs We Don't See," *Eater* (online), May 30, 2018, www.eater.com/2018/5/30/17397060/women-chefs-food-media.

McKibben, Bill. "The End of the World As We Know It," *TLS,* July 31, 2020, pp. 4–5.

McWilliams, James E. *A Revolution in Eating: How the Quest for Food Shaped America* (New York: Columbia University Press, 2005).

Muckenhoupt, Meg. *The Truth About Baked Beans: An Edible New England History* (New York: New York University Press, 2020).

Nestle, Marion. *Food Politics: How the Food Industry Influences Nutrition and Health,* 2nd ed. (Berkeley and Los Angeles: University of California Press, 2007).

Neuhaus, Jessamyn. *Manly Meals and Mom's Home Cooking: Cookbooks and Gender in Modern America* (Baltimore: John Hopkins University Press, 2003).

Parkin, Katherine J. *Food Is Love: Advertising and Gender Roles in Modern America* (Philadelphia: University of Pennsylvania Press, 2006).

Patterson, Orlando. *The Confounding Island: Jamaica and the Post-Colonial Predicament* (Cambridge, Mass.: Harvard University Press, 2019).

Pépin, Jacques. *The Apprentice: My Life in the Kitchen* (Boston: Houghton Mifflin 2003).

Perkins, Blake. "Authenticity and Appropriation: The Southern United States and Scotland," *Petits Propos Culinaires* 166 (2020), 26–45.

Pilgrim, Danya M. "Masters of a Craft: Philadelphia's Black Public Waiters, 1820–50," *Pennsylvania Magazine of History and Biography* 142 (2018), pp. 269–293.

Pollan, Michael. *In Defense of Food: An Eater's Manifesto* (New York: Penguin, 2008).

Purdy, Chase. *Billion Dollar Burger: Inside Big Tech's Race for the Future of Food* (New York: Penguin, 2020).

Records of the Zodiac as They Appear in the Minute Books, 1868–1915 (New York: Privately printed, 1916).

Roberts, Molly. "The Rise and Fall of Alison Roman," *Washington Post,* May 13, 2020, https://www.washingtonpost.com/opinions/2020/05/13/rise-fall-alison-roman.

Rosenbaum, Nancy. "Introduction: Paths to Witnessing, Ethics of Speaking Out," *Daedalus: Journal of the American Academy of Arts and Sciences* 149, no. 4 (Fall 2020), 6–24.

Sabin, Paul. *The Bet: Paul Ehrlich, Julian Simon, and Our Gamble Over Earth's Future* (New Haven: Yale University Press, 2013).

Sahlins, Marshall. *Stone Age Economics* (Chicago: University of Chicago Press, 1972).

Scott, James C. *Against the Grain: A Deep History of the Earliest States* (New Haven: Yale University Press, 2017).

Scrinis, Gyorgy. *Nutritionism: The Science and Politics of Dietary Advice* (New York: Columbia University Press, 2013).

Shapiro, Laura. *Something from the Oven: Reinventing Dinner in 1950s America* (New York: Penguin, 2004).

Sharpless, Rebecca. *Cooking in Other Women's Kitchens: Domestic Workers in the South, 1865–1960* (Chapel Hill: University of North Carolina Press, 2010).

Shields, David S. *The Culinarians: Lives and Careers from the First Age of American Fine Dining* (Chicago: University of Chicago Press, 2017).

Simmel, George. "Sociology of the Meal," *Societies* 37 (1992), 211–216.

Sissons, Michael, and Philip French, eds. *The Age of Austerity, 1945–1951* (Harmondsworth: Penguin, 1963).

Sutton, David E. *Remembrance of Repasts: An Anthropology of Food and Memory* (Oxford: Berg, 2001).

Swislocki, Mark. *Culinary Nostalgia: Regional Food Culture and the Urban Experience in Shanghai* (Stanford: Stanford University Press, 2009).

Tipton-Martin, Toni. *The Jemima Code: Two Centuries of African American Cookbooks* (Austin: University of Texas Press, 2015).

Twitty, Michael W. *The Cooking Gene: A Journey Through African American Culinary History in the Old South* (New York: HarperCollins, 2017).

Vilar, Pierre. *Procès històric i cultura catalana: Reflexions crítiques sobre la cultura catalana* (Barcelona: Generalitat de Catalunya, 1983).

Wallace, Benjamin. "When Restaurants Closed, They Cooked for Each Other," *New York*, April 13–26, 2020, pp. 40–43, 85.

Wallach, Jennifer Jensen. *Every Nation Has Its Dish: Black Bodies and Black Food in Twentieth-Century America* (Chapel Hill: University of North Carolina Press, 2019).

Warner, Valentine. *The Consolation of Food: Stories About Life and Death Seasoned with Recipes* (London: Pavilion Books, 2019).

Waters, Alice. *Coming to My Senses: The Making of a Counterculture Cook* (New York: Clarkson Potter, 2017).

Weber, Elke U. "Seeing Is Believing: Understanding & Aiding Human Responses to Global Climate Change," *Daedalus: Journal of the American Academy of Arts and Sciences* 149, no. 4 (2020), 139–150.

Welch, Deshler. *The Bachelor and the Chafing Dish* (New York and London: F. Tennyson Neely, 1895).

index

chicken, fried, 138

Child, Julia, 37

Childs (restaurant chain), 119–20

chili peppers, 127

China, 28, 30, 66, 172, 177–78; attitudes toward food, 5–6; cuisine of, in United States, 77–78; immigrants from, 12, 77–79, 142; and Muslim Uyghurs, 58; peasant labor in agriculture, 14; rice cultivation in, 24, 170

Chinese Exclusion Act, 78–79, 142

Chinese restaurants, 12, 78–79, 82, 121

Chiquart, Master, 26

Chittenden, Russell, 95

chocolate, 66–68

cholera, 92

Chop Suey Craze, 78

Christianity, 45, 48–58

Christina "the Astonishing" (saint), 54

Churchill, Winston, 158

civil rights movement, 140

clams, 6, 128, 141, 183

climate change, 41, 173–74, 182–85

coffee, 66–67, 68

Columbo's (Nashville), 147

Coming to My Senses: The Making of a Counterculture Cook (Waters), 39, 40

commensality, 151–62

Company (musical), 157

Confounding Island, The (Patterson), 66

Congo, 171

Conklin, Harold, 177

Consolation of Food, The (Warner), 15

Convention on Biodiversity, 172

cookbooks: in the Abbasid Caliphate, 6–7; African American, 138–39; aimed at pleasing husbands, 111; of confectionary recipes, 107; Creole, 145; by Jewish women in Theresienstadt, 4–5; by Massimo Bottura, 116; by Master Chiquart, 26; medieval, 64; pre-Civil War, 109–10; by Sacchi, 35–36; written for men, 112

cooking. *See* food preparation

Cooking Gene, The (Twitty), 139

Cooper, Susan, 180

corn, 128–29, 141

Corrections, The (Franzen), 154

Cota, Rodrigo, 56

Cotton Club (Harlem), 159

Count of Monte Cristo, The (Dumas), 32–33

courtship, 156

Covid-19 pandemic, 4, 20, 69, 160, 165–66, 174, 182, 184

crab cakes, 127

crabs, 6, 53, 127, 132, 134, 135

cranberries, 128, 141, 183

Crete, 15

Croatia, 75

Culinarians, The (Shields), 115

culinary appropriation, 84–85

culinary Luddism, 185–86

culinary modernism, 186

cultural efflorescence, 25

culture, 16

curry restaurants, 79

Vauxhall Gardens (London), 108
veganism, 59, 113
vegetarianism, 40, 113, 125; for
  environmental reasons, 59; for
  health reasons, 59; for moral
  reasons, 59; and religion, 46, 47,
  59
Versailles, palace of, 159
Vilar, Pierre, 11
Virginia Housewife (Randolph),
  143
vitamin C, 95
Volstead Act, 121
Voltaire, 66

Wall Street (film), 31
Warner, Valentine, 15
Washington, Booker T., 137
waste, 27
water depletion and pollution, 169
watering holes, 159
watermelon, 126
Waters, Alice, 37, 38, 39, 40, 115,
  116
Weber, Elke U., 185
Welch, Deshler, 112
Wells, H. G., 119
West Indies, 125–27, 132
Western Reserve University
  (Cleveland), 110

white superiority, 142–43
wild greens, 127
Williams, Sarah Frances Hicks,
  130–31
Winchell, Walter, 159
wine, 129
Wittgenstein, Ludwig, 6, 30
Woloson, Wendy A, 108
women: as chefs, 115–16; and
  commensality, 157–58; food
  preferences of, 106–8, 110–12; and
  food preparation, 103–6, 152; as
  restaurant patrons, 117–21
Woman's Education Association, 96,
  137
Woods, Sylvia, 115
World Trade Organization, 173

yams, 126
Yankee cakes, 143
yellow fever, 92
Yellow Peril, 142
Yemen, 21
*You'll Never Eat Lunch in This Town
  Again* (Phillips), 160
Yuppies, 78

Zhang Dai, 6
Zodiac Club, 34
Zuni, 38

Paul Freedman is the Chester D. Tripp Professor of History at Yale University. His teaching and research concentrate on the history of the Middle Ages (particularly in Catalonia) and the history of food and cuisine. In 2007 Freedman edited *Food: The History of Taste,* which has been translated into ten languages. He is the author of *Ten Restaurants That Changed America* (2016) and *American Cuisine and How It Got This Way* (2019).

Featuring intriguing pairings of authors and subjects, each volume in the **Why X Matters** series presents a concise argument for the continuing relevance of an important idea.

Also in the series: